Praise for *Seeing Right*

Smart, accessible, and richly textured, *Seeing Right* rightly places aesthetics at the heart of Evangelical spiritual and cultural formation. An essential contribution to the study of American Evangelicalism.

—Kristin Kobes Du Mez, *New York Times* bestselling author of *Jesus and John Wayne: How White Evangelicals Corrupted a Faith and Fractured a Nation*

Evangelicals in the United States appear to many as a confused and confusing lot, in large part because some who identify as Evangelical endorse a variety of political projects and societal practices that directly undermine the very religious convictions they claim to hold so dear. In *Seeing Right*, Jason Fallin provides both a helpful diagnosis and a possible prescription for the root cause of this seeming contradiction. For good and for ill, Evangelicals understand and interpret their world not in terms of ethical philosophy, or politics, or even theology, but primarily on aesthetic grounds. Fallin rightly points out that, to overlook the aesthetic dimensions of the Evangelical vision is not only to mis-diagnose its problematic tendencies and entertain unworkable alternatives. It is also to fail, ourselves, to see the world rightly.

—Kutter Callaway, associate professor of theology and culture, Fuller Seminary, and author of *The Aesthetics of Atheism: Theology and Imagination in Contemporary Culture*

In this important book, Jason Fallin convincingly shows that aesthetics is fundamental to moral formation and the practices of the good life. He argues that aesthetics is not only about art work and museums; it also expresses our feelings for the world and each other.

I0894462

Making use of Operation Christmas Child, K-Love, and Evangelical filmmaking, Fallin powerfully illustrates how the Evangelical aesthetic shapes moral imagination in ways that neither contribute to the formation of virtue nor resonate with the common good.

—William Dyrness, senior professor of theology and culture, Fuller Theological Seminary, and author most recently of *The Facts on the Ground: A Wisdom Theology of Culture* (2022)

It is common to understand evangelicalism in terms of its historical lineage, theological emphases, or political configurations. But Jason Fallin argues that we must also reckon with its aesthetic experience: the cultivation of common sentiment through material culture and formative practice. For anyone who has listened to K-Love or filled shoeboxes for Operation Christmas Child, Fallin's book is a fascinating exploration of how evangelicals are oriented to sense and survey the world. Fallin is incisive but not reductive, discerning but not dismissive. He invites all Christians to consider how we are shaped to love what we love and how we are shaped to show it.

—Justin Ariel Bailey, professor of theology, Dordt University, and author of *Interpreting Your World: Five Lenses for Engaging Theology and Culture*

Seeing Right

Seeing RIGHT

Evangelicals and the Aesthetics of Virtue and Vice

Jason M. R. Fallin

FORTRESS PRESS
MINNEAPOLIS

SEEING RIGHT
Evangelicals and the Aesthetics of Virtue and Vice

30 29 28 27 26 25 2 3 4 5 6 7 8 9

Library of Congress Control Number: 2025930582 (print)

Cover image: Fully blurred photograph of a colorful stained glass window depicting Jesus Christ in Combloux, Haute-Savoie, France - stock photo by Colors Hunter - Chasseur de Couleurs/Getty Images
Cover design: Kristin Miller

Print ISBN: 978-1-5064-9945-1
eBook ISBN: 978-1-5064-9946-8

To Erika, Orion, and Maddie

Contents

Acknowledgments

This book is the product of years of internal conversations, false starts, anxious moments sitting in front of unfinished paragraphs, and long hours. It is also the product of the support of, encouragement of, and conversations with friends, family, and colleagues. This is witness to the notion that projects like this are not the work of one person alone but incorporate the contributions of many. As such, I feel that simple expressions of thanks are inadequate to articulate my feelings of indebtedness and gratitude for all those who have offered assistance, advice, and comfort along the way. Nevertheless, I will do my best to articulate my gratitude.

I would first like to acknowledge and thank my wife Erika and my children Orion and Madeleine for their constant love, patience, and encouragement. These pages would not exist without their assistance in carving out the time for writing. I would also like to acknowledge the love and support of my father Michael Fallin, my mother Marcia Tipton, and my father-in-law Frank Randall. I would like to thank professors Bill Dyrness and Hak Joon Lee for their oversight of the research that represents the foundation of this book. Their challenges and critiques greatly improved my scholarship and writing. I would also like to acknowledge S. Brent Plate for his help and input relating to early attempts to articulate the aesthetics that lie at the heart of this project. I would like to thank my colleagues from the Fellowship for Protestant Ethics, and in particular those that helped to workshop an early chapter of this book. In addition, I must thank Justin Bailey and Joshua Beckett for their ongoing encouragement and friendship.

I would also like to thank the communities that encouraged me and my family as this work was being completed. I would like to thank the late great Intentional Community at Madison Square in Pasadena. Living life among these fellow students and their families has been one of the most meaningful experiences of my life. I would like to thank Grace Brethren Church of Calvert County, Pasadena Covenant Church, and Grace Church at West Shore for allowing me to minister through music and word. Their community, ministry, and fellowship has proven a great source of strength and comfort for me and my family. I must also thank Pastor Jay McKinley in particular for his encouragement, prayer, and conversations.

Many thanks to Bethany Dickerson for her faith in this project, for her editorial insights, and for her assistance in finding the voice of this project. I would also like to thank the entire team at Fortress Press for their assistance from proposal to published product.

Finally, I would like to thank all those who have cultivated and nurtured my love for theology, the arts, and culture. In particular, my thanks go out to Chris Garrett and John Heusted for the music, fellowship, and friendship that have cultivated these loves for more than thirty years. This book would not exist without you.

CHAPTER ONE

Evangelicalism and Aesthetic Formation

What Is at Stake?

> Love as our most fundamental orientation to the world—is less a conscious choice and more like a baseline inclination, a default orientation that generates the choices we make.
>
> —James K. A. Smith, *You Are What You Love: The Spiritual Power of Habit*

During an interview in 2023 theologian and ethicist Russell Moore recounted speaking to a pastor who had recently preached on Jesus's Sermon on the Mount and had spent some time considering Jesus's imperative to turn the other cheek if slapped.[1] After the service a parishioner asked where the pastor had received his liberal talking points. When told that turning the other cheek was a quotation directly attributed to Jesus in the Gospels, the man replied, "Yes, but that doesn't work anymore. That's weak."[2] Moore goes on, "When we

1 See Matt 5:38, 39.

2 Scott Detrow, Gabriel J. Sánchez, and Sarah Handel, "He Was a Top Church Official Who Criticized Trump. He Says Christianity Is in Crisis," *NPR.com*, August 8, 2023, https://www.npr.org/2023/08/08/1192663920/southern-baptist-convention-donald-trump-christianity.

[Evangelicals] get to the point where the teachings of Jesus himself are seen as subversive to us, then we're in a crisis."[3] Moore may be right about the crisis; however, the nature of that crisis may be different than is commonly believed. For example, Moore believes this crisis is rooted in disconnection, loneliness, and a sense of alienation.[4] While he aptly names some of the crisis's symptoms, one must dig deeper to find to find its roots. The crisis is instead at least partially rooted in perception, or more specifically the processes that form the meaning we make of what we see, taste, touch, taste, and feel. The crisis is aesthetic.

Humans are all formed by their loves and affections, and those loves are formed by aesthetic processes. These aesthetic processes are fundamental to the formation of faith, and the demonstration of those loves and affections represent a fundamental part of being human. Human practices are shaped by and grow out of the soil of the objects, ideas, and people that we love. These loves and the practices they nurture frame notions of identity and self-understanding. They provide a framework for answering some of the biggest questions about who we are and how we fit into the social structures in which we are embedded.

The commitment that affections and aesthetics are connected is followed closely by a second commitment that aesthetic texts (such as art, movies, television shows, music, and social media) and material culture (such as tools, buildings, documents, furniture, memorials, and clothes) play an essential role in the cultivation of our loves and affections and the practices stirred by our affections. These represent an interplay between one's loves and affections and the loves and affections of others. Finally, both of these commitments are rooted in a larger theological commitment that this formation of human practices by way of the formation of human affections is fundamental to the human experience and is particularly essential to the experience of embodiment. Moreover, this embodiment represents a divine gift, and thus a divine good. The body represents the material in which the

3 Detrow et al., "He Was a Top Church Official."

4 Detrow et al., "He Was a Top Church Official."

imago Dei (the image of God) is embedded in every human. Furthermore, the affections rooted in our embodiment also represent a divine gift and a divine good, also representing a portion of the *imago Dei*. In short, just as God is revealed as both rational and affective, so, as image bearers, humans are also revealed as both as well.

While these aesthetic formations play out in every person's life, they are markedly present in the white Evangelical community in the United States and in the processes that have formed their affections and practices over the past several decades. Naming and highlighting these aesthetic processes help us to understand how they aided in the formation of a community that produced the Moral Majority in the 1980s and the mantra "character matters" in the 1990s, and also fostered a community that broadly supports and defends a man like Donald Trump whose practices, rhetoric, and lifestyle seem inconsistent with the character and values that Evangelicals have historically advocated.[5] In the wake of the Trump presidency, many have endeavored to account for moral formation among white

5 The Pew Research Center notes that 77 percent of white Protestants who identified themselves as Evangelical voted for Donald Trump in 2016, and 84 percent voted for him in 2020. See Justin Nortey, "Most White Americans Who Regularly Attend Worship Services Voted for Trump in 2020," Pew Research Center, August 30, 2021, https://www.pewresearch.org/short-reads/2021/08/30/most-white-americans-who-regularly-attend-worship-services-voted-for-trump-in-2020/. A brief condensation of this tension can be seen in the manner in which Evangelical evangelist Franklin Graham characterized the moralities and characters of Presidents Bill Clinton and Donald Trump. Of Clinton he wrote in a *Wall Street Journal* op-ed, "But the God of the Bible says that what one does in private does matter. Mr. Clinton's months-long extramarital sexual behavior in the Oval Office now concerns him and the rest of the world, not just his immediate family. If he will lie to or mislead his wife and daughter, those with whom he is most intimate, what will prevent him from doing the same to the American public?" ("Clinton's Sins Aren't Private," *Wall Street Journal*, August 27, 1998, accessed January 24, 2024, https://www.wsj.com/articles/SB904162265981632000). Of Trump he wrote in a Facebook post, "It is unfortunate that many people got confused and made the election about personalities rather than the policies of the candidates. President Trump will go down in history as one of the great presidents of our nation" (Facebook, December 14, 2020, https://www.facebook.com/FranklinGraham/posts/3957463454309806).

Evangelicals through theological, sociological, political, or anthropological lenses. Each of these provide useful frameworks for understanding the shifts and apparently conflicting formations within the white Evangelical community. Each, however, misses the aesthetic components and processes fundamental to these formations. Thus, any attempt to account for notions of identity and formation among humans broadly, and among white Evangelicals in particular, must include an aesthetic component in order to provide a holistic and thick account of that identity and formation.

These commitments to and interests in the aesthetic roots of formation are representative of what can be called an aesthetic turn in theology over the past several decades, as Christian theologians and ethicists have signaled an interest in the role played by the aesthetic, the body, and the affections in the formation of Christian discipleship and practices. The result has been a greater focus on the role played by the interaction of embodiment and material culture in theological and ethical discourse. Continuing in that vein, aesthetic and affective processes represent essential contributions to the formation of the individual's loves and imagination and subsequently to their spiritual and moral formation. Therefore aesthetic texts and the practices associated with those texts represent a key component of human moral formation. The observations related to the relationship between aesthetics and practices will produce an accurate sketch of the aesthetic processes that are fundamental to moral formation.

THE FORMATIONAL STAKES—WHY AESTHETICS?

Some may ask why this aesthetic approach to describing moral formation is necessary. It is necessary because the theological, sociological, anthropological, and political approaches, while valuable, fail to devote sufficient attention to the role that the body and the affections play in moral formation. And while the anthropological approach is concerned with the relationship between material culture and practices, its adherents are not generally concerned with the aesthetic processes by which aesthetic texts and material culture form affections that then express themselves through practices. In contrast, the aesthetic approach seeks to connect the affections of the body, resulting in a performance of practices, to the theological, philosophical, political, and ideological commitments embedded in aesthetic texts and material culture. Perhaps the culturally suspicious Christians who warned the church a generation ago of the dangers of "Garbage In, Garbage Out" may have hit closer to the mark than some may have wanted to believe, though likely in ways they would not have or could not have foreseen. In short what is at stake is the theological understanding of the roles the body, the materiality in which the body is embedded, and performance play in moral formation. At stake as well is a model of moral formation that accounts for the roles of culture, perception, imagination, and performance as part of the formational webs in which every human is embedded.

The theological and formational implications of the stakes are far-reaching. To understand the formational implications of aesthetic texts, look to advertising and its pithy and punchy use of aesthetic texts in commercials. Marketers understand the fundamental role the body plays in the formation of our affections. The viewer sees, reads, and hears the sales pitch in the commercial as it provokes and arouses the viewer's affections. In the television show *Mad Men*, Don Draper works in advertising. During a sales pitch where he is marketing new carousel slide projectors to Kodak, he tells their executives, "The most important idea in advertising is 'new.' It creates an itch." Don then talks about a deeper bond with the product: nostalgia. Draper shares slides of happy images of his own family through the projector (the narrative of the show is simultaneously juxtaposing these images against the reality of his family's brokenness). He goes on, "This device isn't a space ship. It's a time machine. It goes backwards; forwards. It takes us to a place we ache to go again. It's not called the wheel, it's called a carousel. It lets us travel the way a child travels, round and around, back home again, to a place we know we are loved."[6] The writers of *Mad Men* dramatically reveal the persuasive potential aesthetic texts and material culture instantiate. These ads aim to form the participant's affections by means of their senses, and thus through their bodies.

Advertisers appeal to affections because the body is both fundamental to moral formation and necessary to enact the practices they are persuading you to perform. Advertisements promote a particular set of practices, such as buying burgers, diamonds, or cars, or donating money or resources toward a particular charity, or joining a branch of the military. Each wants our bodies to perform certain sets of practices as a result of their aesthetic text. In the process, ads must work to form our affections and imaginations to such an extent that we carry this formation into our practices.

This embodied storage of affections is part and parcel of the relationships among materiality, corporeality, and moral formation, or perhaps better said, of the formation of virtues. However, because of its embodied, affective nature these formational processes can result in the formation of what we might call unvirtuous virtues. If each of these aesthetic texts instantiate particular visions of the good life, the formation of unvirtuous virtues would mean pointing those visions toward ends that some would deem harmful. An example would be aesthetic texts that persuade people with addiction disorders to participate in gambling, the consumption of alcohol, or social media. Not every vision of the good life represents the actual good life.

Within a Christian community, Scripture and tradition represent the notions the good life are constructed around. Theologian and ethicist Stanley Hauerwas frames the good life as the Christian embedded in a Christian community and participating in the story of God, particularly as that story is articulated in the Gospels.[7] The community then passes along their readings and interpretations of

---

6 *Mad Men*, season 1, episode 13, directed by Matthew Weiner, aired October 18, 2007 on AMC.

7 Stanley Hauerwas, *The Peaceable Kingdom: A Primer in Christian Ethics* (University of Notre Dame Press, 1983), 62.

that narrative to the newer members of the community as they retell that story. This allows for a broad variety of interpretations and narrative emphases to be passed on by the multitude of Christian communities. At its best, within a Christian context, this process results in what Hauerwas envisions as a servant community that manifests the peaceable kingdom of God pictured in the Gospels.[8] At its worst it allows for the creation and perpetuation of practices and habits that, even as they are framed as embodying that servant community, are in fact embodying the opposite. In the cases of both advertising and the church, the affective nature of this formation leaves space for notions of both formation and malformation.

Every vision of the good life exists among a significant number of competing visions of the good life. These competing visions do not just exist within the broader culture. They also exist among other Christian organizations and within the church itself. Because of this, the formation that occurs (among Evangelicals, for example) represents only a partial formation. Humans are always subject to analogous and contradictory formations. They are always simultaneously confronted with multiple visions of the good life through the aesthetic texts and pieces of material culture they are engaging. Thus, the formation that occurs in the individual through their aesthetic engagements is always provisional and reversible in light of the persuasive power of the competing aesthetic texts and the material culture they engage. Aesthetic formation is durable, because of its embeddedness in the individual's affections, dispositions, and practices; however, it is not permanent, as one can come to love and perform counternarratives that undermine one's affections and what can be called their primary formational narratives. This is part of the reason why marketers are consistently creating new aesthetic texts. They recognize their brand must consistently renew that vision in order to form the practices and actions of viewers and readers.

Understanding aesthetic formation is rooted in a particular theology of the body. Because aesthetic formation is rooted in the body

8 Hauerwas, *Peaceable Kingdom*, 99.

and that body is rooted in the materiality of the world, any discourse accounting for that formation is rooted in a particular theology of creation. This particular theology of creation values creation as a material expression of divine love and believes it represents a divine project that humans are invited to participate in and contribute to.[9] More importantly, this theology of creation frames creation as a space in which humans were designed not only to exist, but to thrive. Thus the formation occurring as the individual interacts with aesthetic texts is fundamental to the experience of existing as a human designed to live in a material and thus an aesthetic environment. In addition, the formation represents not only ethical and aesthetic processes, but also theological processes. The processes are fundamental to the manner in which humans are created, and as such these processes are theological because they describe processes embedded in humanity by God. Because of this, aesthetic formation represents a theological inquiry as much as it does an ethical and aesthetic inquiry.

Articulating a relationship between aesthetic texts and practices shapes an understanding of practices and performances in two ways. The first revolves around the potentially diagnostic use of practices and performance for assessing the effects of a given aesthetic formational process. If human practices are representing enactments of a

9 This commitment is rooted both in God's gifting of the *imago Dei* to humanity, and to what is often described as the cultural mandate given to humanity is Gen 1:26–28. ("Then God said, 'Let us make mankind in our image, in our likeness, so that they may rule over the fish in the sea and the birds in the sky, over the livestock and all the wild animals, and over all the creatures that move along the ground.' So God created mankind in his own image, in the image of God he created them; male and female he created them. God blessed them and said to them, 'Be fruitful and increase in number; fill the earth and subdue it. Rule over the fish in the sea and the birds in the sky and over every living creature that moves on the ground'" [NIV].) William Dyrness in *The Earth Is God's: A Theology of American Culture* (Wipf & Stock Publishers, 1997), describes this theological commitment well: "God works in and with creation in grace and judgment. The human creature is called to work with God on this project both with and on behalf of the rest of creation. For it is only in relation to God's presence and work in creation that the creature finds its meaning" (26).

person's aesthetic commitments, then those practices can be a means of assessing the trajectory of an individual's formation, particularly as that assessment is done alongside the aesthetic texts funding that formation. James K. A. Smith may assert in his book title that *You Are What You Love*, but if an individual's loves and affections contribute to the formation of their actions and practices then we can also argue that "You are what you do." One's actions represent performances of one's affections and dispositions.

The second implication revolves around the aesthetic nature of performance. If the enactment of practices represent aesthetic texts available to the senses of others, and aesthetic texts can provoke and form imaginations and dispositions, then the dramatic performances of individuals and communities contribute to aesthetic formation. In short, one's own performances participate in the formational processes of others, both inside and outside of that individual's community. This is because the body represents its own aesthetic text. There is a certain social persuasion in a community engaging in a set of practices. This social pressure is often colloquially framed in terms of peer pressure—that is, the expected practical conformity to particular sets of social norms, or social scripts. However, because the aesthetic embodies particular social forces this pressure, for lack of a better word, is itself an aesthetic force, or at the very least can be said to embody a certain type of aesthetic discourse.

Hauerwas touches on the aesthetic nature of performance when he argues that character is a gift from the community. He contends that Christians attract others to God's story of peace as they perform that story in their common life.[10] This is true both for those who are members of the Christian community as Hauerwas envisions it and for those outside of that community.[11] The Christian observes the performances of the other Christians in the community in which she is embedded, particularly the performances of those whose characters best represent the story of God's peace as that is framed by

10 Hauerwas, *The Peaceable Kingdom*, 44.
11 Hauerwas, *The Peaceable Kingdom*, 45.

the community. That performance behaves as its own aesthetic text, working to form the affections and imaginations of the ones engaging that performance.[12] Thus performance is not just an expression of the aesthetic formation that has occurred in an individual or community; it is also contributing to the further aesthetic formation of the community. Practices are therefore as fundamental as the texts themselves in the process of aesthetic formation.

WHOSE AESTHETICS?

The word *aesthetic* carries in it a wide array of meanings. Theologian Richard Viladesau helps denote the potential scope of the notion of the aesthetic: "'Aesthetics' may be understood as practice (art) and as theory. It can refer to a number of overlapping subjects, including art, symbol, feeling, beauty, taste, imagination, and perception. A theological or religious aesthetics considers any of these topics in the light of God, revelation, and the sacred." Furthermore, "[Aesthetics] could refer to the philosophy of beauty, the laws of sensible perception, the study of art, the phenomenon of taste, or the active appreciation of beauty."[13] Viladesau's description underlines two points. First, he highlights that at its core the aesthetic can be framed as the space where sensible perception and culture intertwine. Even if one chooses to engage only the notions of sensible perception and leave aside the notion of the aesthetic as a philosophy of beauty, for example, one must still account for the role culture and the social

12 On a side note, I believe this is something similar to what Paul is describing in 2 Corinthians 3: "You are our epistle written in our hearts, known and read by all men; clearly you are an epistle of Christ, ministered by us, written not with ink but by the Spirit of the living God, not on tablets of stone but on tablets of flesh, that is, of the heart" (2 Cor 3:2–3 NKJV). Paul is writing of the persuasive power of bodies and performance.

13 Richard Viladesau, "Aesthetics and Religion," in *The Oxford Handbook of Religion and the Arts*, ed. Frank Burch Brown (Oxford University Press, 2014), 25.

body play in the interpretation of that sensible perception. Second, Viladesau highlights just how much meaning the term *aesthetic* has accrued over the years, expanding to cover a significant amount of semantic ground.

For the purposes of considering the processes fundamental to aesthetic formation, the word *aesthetic* cannot be allowed to cover that much semantic ground. Instead I intend to largely consider the aesthetic as sensible perception. To that end, I will focus on aesthetic discourse relating to the senses and subsequently to perception. While I will not primarily be engaging in conversations relating to philosophies of art and beauty, or to taste, ancillary conversations relating to taste will be inevitable and necessary because of the manner in which they are formed through the senses. By homing in on this particular segment of aesthetic discourse, I will provide a sketch of the relationship between the senses and perception and thus the formation of the imagination and dispositions.

Aesthetics as Sensible Perception

Visual culture scholar David Morgan provides a useful starting point for describing this approach to the aesthetic. He defines the aesthetic as the "sensuous, imagined, embodied experience of meaning whose significance is measured in feeling no less than intellectual content."[14] This approach is more interested in discourse related to meaning, particularly as it is constructed out of embodied experience, than it is interested in discourse related, for example, to taste. Morgan's rooting of the aesthetic first in the senses means we must spend some time describing something of those meaning-making processes before describing their relations to the experience related to aesthetic texts themselves. Here, philosopher Mark Johnson is particularly helpful in articulating the relationship of the body to the aesthetic.

14 David Morgan, "Protestant Visual Piety and the Aesthetics of American Mass Culture," in *Mediating Religion*, ed. Jolyon Mitchell and Sophia Marriage (T&T Clark, 2003), 107.

Johnson begins his approach to the aesthetic with the thesis that "what we call 'mind' and what we call 'body' are not two things, but rather aspects of one organic process, so that all our meaning, thought, and language emerge from the aesthetic dimensions of this embodied activity."[15] Using this approach Johnson intends to counter the modernist approach to epistemology, which creates a strong duality between the mind and the body. Instead Johnson argues that the meaning constructed by humans grows first out of the interaction between the physical world and the body.[16] For Johnson, both reason and imagination are framed as simultaneously affective and bodily processes.[17] Leaning on the pragmatism of William James and James Dewey, Johnson understands the mind as "a process of organism-environment interactions."[18] Thus he can argue, for example, that reason represents "only embodied *processes* by which our experience

---

15 Mark Johnson, *The Meaning of the Body: Aesthetics of Human Understanding* (University of Chicago Press, 2007), 1.

16 Thus he writes, "The key to my entire argument is that meaning is not just what is consciously entertained in acts of feeling and thought; instead, meaning reaches deep down into our corporeal encounter with our environment." (Johnson, *Meaning of the Body*, 25).

17 On this point, Johnson cites the work of neuroscientist Antonio Damasio, who provides an account of emotions rooted both in ecology and evolutionary science: "The primary task for any organism—the task that must be accomplished before all others—is the preservation of life and the furtherance of conditions for the organism's growth" (*Meaning of the Body*, 55). He goes on to note that humans have "developed a large ensemble of interrelated systems . . . geared toward our continued existence, growth and flourishing" (55). Among these systems are emotions and feelings. He goes on to note that the human body is always tuned into its environment, assessing the constant flow of experience for threats that when perceived trigger the emotions to facilitate the survival of the organism. Thus, "Emotional responses can occur long before we become aware that we are *feeling* an emotion. Since feelings are consciously experienced bodily processes, while emotional responses can operate beneath the level of consciousness, feeling cannot be a necessary condition for an emotional response, even though feeling typically, and importantly, does accompany the emotional response" (59). Because reason is born out of the affectivity of experience, its roots can be said themselves to be fundamentally affective.

18 Johnson, *Meaning of the Body*, 117.

is explored, criticized and transformed in inquiry."[19] Likewise imagination is also rooted in bodily processes that make new meaning, expand and extend concepts to new contexts, and creatively find new ways to make sense of new experiences.[20] He goes on to argue that the meaning that humans make from and of these flows of experience are socially constructed, reflecting cultural, religious, and community values, commitments and practices.[21] He writes,

> The reduction of the body to the mere physical organism is just as misguided as the error of claiming the body is nothing but a cultural construct. They are both reductions; the first leaves out large parts of what makes meaning and mind possible, and the second leaves out many of the sources of, and constraints on, meaning and mind that come from the character of our corporeal rootedness in the biological-ecological processes of life.[22]

If Johnson's general framework is correct then all human meaning making is fundamentally embodied and thus entirely dependent upon sensible perception.

In *The Sacred Gaze*, David Morgan takes a similar approach to the aesthetic, though without the emphasis on neuroscience. As Johnson did, Morgan begins this project of accounting for the formational role sight plays by also affirming that the body and the mind are

---

19 Johnson, *Meaning of the Body*, 13. Reason is framed here as "an accomplishment of inquiry" as opposed to "a pre-given fact or capacity" (13). Thus Johnson argues that reason cannot exist independent of embodiment.

20 Johnson, *Meaning of the Body*, 13.

21 Johnson, *Meaning of the Body*, 151. Writing of the social construction of the mind that precedes the construction of meaning, Johnson argues, "[The mind] emerges as, and is enacted through, social cognition. I think it is therefore accurate to say that we are not born with minds fully formed and ready for thinking. Instead, we acquire 'minds' through our coordinated sharing of meaning and our concomitant ability to engage in symbolic interactions" (151). Pushing this point a bit further, Johnson argues, leaning on Maurice Merleau-Ponty, that the body that constructs this meaning is in reality many bodies intermingled. He recognizes that the body is a biological organism, but that it is simultaneously an ecological body, a phenomenological body, a social body, and a cultural body (275–77).

22 Johnson, *Meaning of the Body*, 277, 278.

not separate entities.[23] He goes on to argue that sight is not simply a biological function, but also an assemblage of habit and social construction.[24] Morgan's book provides an account of this simultaneously social and visual (think embodied) construction of the sacred. In light of the social processes that contribute to the formation of vision, Morgan writes, "One bears on one's body the signs of participation in the social body and one inhabits this body by seeing with its eyes, smelling with its olfaction, feeling with its fingers and flesh. The fact that human beings are always seer and seen, agent and the object of vision, means that the individual human body is not only a discrete biological unit, but also a medium, an interface, the way we participate in bodies larger than our own."[25] He goes on to argue that vision must be understood as an act occurring with the entire body of the seer; that is, the seer sees simultaneously with their biological body, and as a member of particular social bodies.[26] Because this act of sight is fully embodied, he argues that the image by its nature then moves us toward the body, toward feeling and affect. In this way the body and the image are a bonded pair.[27] Therefore, within Morgan's framework, any engagement of a particular aesthetic text or piece of material culture, be it fine art, popular art, or a work of craft, regardless of which senses are employed for that engagement, is fully embodied; that is, there is no active sense that is not engaged as one gives active attention to that piece of material culture. Because

---

23 David Morgan, *The Sacred Gaze: Religious Visual Culture in Theory and Practice* (University of California Press, 2004), 2.

24 Morgan, *The Sacred Gaze*, 74.

25 David Morgan, *The Embodied Eye: Religious Visual Culture and the Social Life of Feeling* (University of California Press, 2012), 6.

26 Morgan, *The Embodied Eye*, 15.

27 Morgan, *The Embodied Eye*, 30. Acknowledging the historical-theoretical connection of touching and seeing (he cites those wary of images from Plato to Calvin, who feared the image's affective power as an indulgence of desire) Morgan references the notion of haptic visuality to describe "a certain powerful mode of vision—seeing that maps the visual terrain in terms of touch, texture, proximity, all sensory features that the hands and the body use to register the material character of something" (111).

of this framework Morgan can position these pieces of material culture as "the cultural productions, circulation, and reception of felt-knowledge."[28]

Another writer who also speaks of the social and thus embodied role of the aesthetic is French philosopher Pierre Bourdieu. Interestingly, he brings the consideration of the aesthetic full circle, endeavoring to account for the role played by the body and the senses in the formation of taste. One of the foundational claims Bourdieu makes is that a person's sense of taste (that is, their disposition toward particular pieces of material culture) is shaped first and foremost by the "elementary taste for the flavours of food."[29] Thus for Bourdieu taste is formed through simultaneously embodied and social processes and most easily perceived in and through an individual's interaction with material culture. Bourdieu argues that an individual's native disposition toward the material is learned and formed first within a familial setting, and is then extended by education.[30] This is why he argues that every person's material inheritance is also a cultural inheritance.[31] Pieces of material culture transmit the virtues, values, and dispositions toward the material that become the essence of taste.[32]

This model of aesthetic discourse—as it relates to sensible perception (as exemplified by these three authors)—constructs an account of how the role aesthetic texts and material culture play in the formation of the individual's and community's affections and dispositions. However, moral formation that stops at the formation of one's affections and dispositions represents a rather incomplete account of that

---

28 Morgan, *The Embodied Eye*, 147.

29 Pierre Bourdieu, *Distinction: A Social Critique of the Judgement of Taste*, trans. Richard Nice (Harvard University Press, 1984), 1. Bourdieu defines taste as "culture turned into nature, that is, *embodied*, helps to shape the class body" (190).

30 Bourdieu, *Distinction*, 66.

31 Bourdieu, *Distinction*, 76.

32 Bourdieu, *Distinction*, 227. Bourdieu would argue that the manner in which an individual appropriates a work of art embodies the relation of distinction particular to his or her taste.

formation. A full account of moral formation also requires the way internal dispositions become externalized into action.

Dramatics and Performance

Practices represent the intended end of aesthetic moral formation. One interested in cultivating a certain set of practices endeavors to first cultivate particular sets of affections, imaginations, and dispositions. To use a metaphor, practices represent the fruit growing from the tree of affections and imaginations. For example, if, sometime after engaging a commercial, you find yourself persuaded to purchase a particular product, you will likely either find yourself at your computer, purchasing it online, or driving to a brick and mortar store. In any case you are viewing and perhaps handling the pieces of material culture available to be purchased, and making judgments as to which pieces are most meaningful to you. Embedded within these acts of perception are particular understandings of what constitutes the good life. As such, these actions represent performances of the narratives that have shaped the participant's perceptive apparatus and imagination. Through these actions the actor offers a glimpse of the shape of the good life that has been formed in his affections. It is only through action that one is ultimately able to see the meaning being constructed by the participant in relation to pieces of material culture. And only through action do the embodied expressions of the actors reveal the narratives that have formed those affections, imaginations, and dispositions. Thus dramatic discourse becomes a vital means of describing the telos of aesthetic discourse and the associated formation of perception.

Discourse related to dramatic theory has not received anywhere near the attention received by aesthetic discourse. In fact, the mantle of dramatic discourse lay largely undisturbed after Aristotle's *Poetics*. This neglect was likely at least partially due to the latent commitment within Mediterranean Christianity to a Neo-platonically shaped theological framework.[33] The critical consideration of theater was not

33 Theatre historian Dale Savidge notes that this Neo-platonic commitment was at least partially responsible for the church's ambivalence, if not outright

taken up again in Western discourse until the birth of the passion plays in the thirteenth century. Indeed the application of dramatic theory to theological discourse only begun in earnest within the past sixty years.[34]

Theologian and liturgist Todd Johnson notes that drama and by extension theater is the only creative genre where stories are told through the medium of people's bodies and actions. It is "a medium through which people—the actors—tell stories by becoming the story."[35] By its nature, the medium transforms the static into the dynamic. Drama converts the image into action and script into performance, and thus can be understood as a space where narrative

hostility, toward the theater. One might be able to make a case that the resurgence of Aristotelian thought in Europe, particularly following Thomas Aquinas, in some ways correlates to the resurgence in the use of theater, particularly as it relates to the manner in which it was employed by the institution of the church. See "A Survey of Christianity and Theatre in History," in *Performing the Sacred: Theology and Theatre in Dialogue*, ed. Todd Eric Johnson and Dale Savidge (Baker Academic, 2009), 32–35.

34 Swiss theologian Hans Urs Von Balthasar is credited as the initiator of this conversation after publishing his five volume *Theo-Drama*. Von Balthasar, building on his seven-volume theological aesthetics *The Glory of the Lord*, wanted to provide a deeply theological account of the transcendental notion of the good. Because of the inherent relationship between the good and the action necessary to bring it about, Von Balthasar chose to employ the framework of dramatic theory to describe the relationship between the divine and human action that brings that good about. For Von Balthasar, the incarnation (Jesus's life, death by crucifixion, and resurrection) represents the action(s) that bring about the divine good. He notes in his pithy meditation on love, *Love Alone Is Credible*, that God's action of revealing the good then lies "solely in God's presentation of himself to human beings on the stage of human nature," a form humanity is able to recognize, and thus through drama (Hans Urs Von Balthasar, *Love Alone Is Credible*, trans. D. C. Schindler [Ignatius Press, 1963], 70). In doing so, Von Balthasar is endeavoring to provide space for both the divine and the human to act freely on what is framed ostensibly as the world stage. Von Balthasar recognized the usefulness presented by theater and dramatic theory for providing a theological account of God's presence and action in the world.

35 Todd E. Johnson, "Doing God's Story: Theatre, Christian Initiation, and Being Human Together," in *Theatrical Theology: Explorations In Performing the Faith*, ed. Wesley Vander Lugt and Trevor Hart (Cascade Books, 2014), 155.

and performance intertwine. Furthermore dramatic discourse renders both action and image simultaneously available to the senses, which allows for an individual's performance to complete the hermeneutic circle, so to speak, and become its own aesthetic text that itself is available to form the perceptions and dispositions of others.

Practices and performance can reveal the formation of the individual's affections and dispositions; moreover, actions and practices simultaneously represent a performance available to the senses that continuously participates in and contributes to the unceasing formation of perception and virtue in the individual and the community. Therefore, dramatic discourse represents a vital participant in the aesthetic processes that is key to understanding moral formation. In revealing the extent to which the formation of perception and performance has occurred through bodies, actions, and practices, dramatic discourse also reveals an aesthetic of performance that fundamentally participates in the dynamic processes that promote the formation of perception and virtue.

Dramatic discourse should be included in this aesthetic conversation because the processes that are fundamental to moral formation include performance. Dramatic discourse seeks to account for action and presence, thus creating a discourse that supplements, strengthens, and completes the aesthetic account of moral formation. Dramatic discourse allows for observation and description of the relationship between performance, narrative, and text, in this case a set of aesthetic texts. The discourse provides tools that allow us to trace a path from aesthetic text, and the narratives embedded in that text, to the formation of the viewer's affections, to the actions the actions those affections fund and inspire.

AESTHETICS AND VIRTUE ETHICS

If there does exist a fundamental relationship between aesthetic texts and moral formation (a connection, if you will, between text and performance), then virtue ethic discourse represents the most fruitful ethical conversation partner or ethical framework to potentially process that connection because of its attentiveness to the role affections play in the formation of virtue.

When a family makes a weekend trip to a big box store (whether the trip is motivated by marketing or not) they are engaging in a set of practices that carry in them a certain vision of the good life. A virtue ethic framework recognizes that the vision of the good life embodied in these practices fundamentally shapes the affections and imaginations of these participants, and thus shapes future practices that are born out of those affections and imagination.

The project of attempting to account for an individual and community's moral formation is not new. Virtue ethic discourse begins more than two millennia ago with Aristotle's *Nicomachean Ethics*. Aristotle endeavored to provide an account of the development of the virtues necessary to constitute a good life in the polis. He articulates the relationship between an individual's and community's sense of virtues and the imagined end or telos that shaped that sense. Aristotle sought to describe the processes through which one becomes virtuous.[36]

Anchoring Aristotle's account of the formation of virtue is the notion of *eudaimonia*. The best contemporary English translation of this as "happiness" is both correct and simultaneously woefully inadequate. For Aristotle, *eudaimonia* represents the telos, the highest good, and best end that he believed drew people toward virtue like gravity.[37] For Aristotle the practices necessary to pursue this good end represented virtue. As Jennifer Herdt notes, for Aristotle, "There is no alternative route to happiness that takes a detour around

36 In particular see book 2 of Aristotle, *The Ethics of Aristotle: The Nicomachean Ethics*, trans. J. A. K. Thomson (Penguin Classics, 1955).

37 Stanley Hauerwas and Charles Pinches, drawing on J. L. Ackrill, frame eudaimonia as "the best possible life." *Christians among the Virtues* (University of Notre Dame Press 1997), 8.

the virtues but nevertheless arrives at the same goal."[38] Important to the idea of eudaimonia is the recognition that Aristotle did not argue for a particular universal telos, such as the sets of universal ethical norms that are often articulated in deontological approaches to ethics, but allowed the telos to be defined both individually and socially. Aristotle recognized that humanity would never coalesce around a comprehensive set of moral principles and thus allowed for the prospect of communities constructing community virtues around community teloi.

The virtues themselves then represent the actions and practices necessary to achieve the good goal that is the telos.[39] However, the virtues are not enacted exclusively through the sheer will of the moral agent, but are acquired over time and thus come to represent tendencies, dispositions, and capacities. They are habituated to the extent that the virtuous person tends to consistently react to similar circumstances with similar actions.[40] These acts that move us from point one to point two represent the sum of the daily choices and repeated practices necessary to the formation of virtue.[41] Though performed by the individual, these practices do not represent the

---

38 Jennifer A. Herdt, *Putting on Virtue: The Legacy of the Splendid Vices* (University of Chicago Press, 2008), 35.

39 Alasdair MacIntyre, *After Virtue: A Study in Moral Theory* (University of Notre Dame Press, 1984) provides a more descriptive definition: "A virtue is an acquired human quality the possession and exercise of which tends to enable us to achieve those goods which are internal to practices and lack of which effectively prevents us from achieving any such goods" (191).

40 Joseph J. Kotva Jr., *The Christian Case for Virtue Ethics* (Georgetown University Press, 1996), 24. Kotva also frames this process of habituation within a tripartite structure: "1) human-nature-as-it-exists; 2) human-nature-as-it-could-be; 3) those habits, capacities, interests, inclinations, precepts, injunctions, and prohibitions that will move us from point one to point two" (17).

41 Martha Nussbaum notes that Aristotle's ethical approach seems best at "capturing the sheer complexity and agonizing difficulty of choosing well." Though it simultaneously describes the manner in which repeated choices to consistently pursue a telos can lead a moral agent to the point of not having to agonize over choices because of the character created in the formational process. Martha Nussbaum, *Love's Knowledge: Essays on Philosophy and Literature* (Oxford University Press, 1990), 55.

individual work of a single moral agent, but represent the work of a moral agent in the midst of a community of moral agents.

Because of the narrative and social aspects inherent in eudaimonia, philosopher and ethicist Alisdair MacIntyre argues that it can only be accomplished as it is embedded within the practices associated with a particular tradition. He writes that the life of virtue embodies three requirements: (1) practice, (2) narrative order, and (3) moral tradition.[42] He further writes that "to enter a practice is to accept the authority of those standards and the inadequacy of my own performance as judged by them. It is to subject my own attitudes, choices, preferences and tastes to the standards which currently and partially define the practice."[43] Aristotle understood that the submission and repetition associated with these practices within the context of particular traditions produces a change in the affection and dispositions. The practitioner develops an affective attachment to the narrative, and to the community and tradition in which it is rooted. In this way, practices can be understood to operate affectively, potentially facilitating shifts in the practitioner's own affections.

The role of the affections is key to the formational aspects of virtue ethics, because as Hauerwas notes, "an ethic of virtue centers on the claim that an agent's being is prior to doing."[44] In this way, their being

---

42 MacIntyre, *After Virtue*, 187. He defines a practice as "any coherent and complex form of socially established cooperative human activity through which goods internal to that form of activity are realized in the course of trying to achieve those standards of excellence which are appropriate to, and partially definitive of, that form of activity, which the result that human powers to achieve excellence, and human conception of the ends and goods involved, are systemically extended" (187).

43 MacIntyre, *After Virtue*, 190.

44 Stanley Hauerwas, *A Community of Character: Toward a Constructive Christian Social Ethic* (University of Notre Dame Press, 1981), 113. Later in this passage Hauerwas goes on to note, "What is significant about us morally is not what we do or do not do, but how we do what we do. A person of virtue is often said to be a person of style or class in that he or she may well do what others do but in a distinctive manner" (113). I argue that Hauerwas's argument regarding the development of an ethical style represents an attempt to account for matters of the formation of dispositions, and perhaps even the formation of

is not set in stone, but is constantly being formed. A person's being for Hauerwas represents the manner in which she is predisposed to perceive cultural and social world in which she is embedded. Framed this way, an agent's actions, as they relate both to the quotidian and the exceptional choices made from day to day, become a matter of instinct and disposition as he develops an affection for the repeated performance of the practices that are shaping him, and for the community and institutions in which they are embedded, and thus an affection for the story or narrative that drives those practices.[45] In this way, the affections that are formed in an individual might be best framed as the soil out of which the virtues grow, and as such it must be tended and cultivated appropriately in order to produce the intended fruit (the telos).

This formation of course is not generated spontaneously within the individual. It must be enacted within the context of a community and its institutions.[46] While the agent bears responsibility for her own actions and formation (that is for her agency) she is simultaneously dependent on the community for the proper formation of that agency.[47]

---

taste from the perspective of an ethicist. As such I believe he is endeavoring to name and account for some of the same formational forces Bourdieu endeavors to account for in *Distinction*.

45 Interestingly, this insight is at the core of Adam Smith's argument in *The Theory of Moral Sentiments*. He goes as far as to make the case, in the universalizing manner endemic to the Enlightenment, that every action taken by the agent proceeds entirely from the affections. Interestingly, he does so without explicitly referencing Aristotelian ethics. See "Part I: Of the Property of Action," in *The Theory of Moral Sentiments* (Amazon Publishing, 2016).

46 Because of the social web inherent to the formation of virtue, it is best understood as a gift from the community. Hauerwas articulates this well when he writes in *The Peacable Kingdom*, "Our character is a gift from others which we learn to claim as our own by recognizing it as a gift. Our freedom is literally in the hands of others. . . . It is from them that I learn the story that gives my life purpose and direction" (45).

47 Of note here, Jennifer Herdt observes that the notion of the agent's dependence on community for the formation of their own virtue reveals a tension and perhaps even a paradox within virtue ethics. Discussing Aristotle's notion of the magnanimous person, which might be framed as one in whom all the potential of virtue has become fully realized in a self-sufficient moral

Virtue ethics implicitly assumes an aesthetic foundation of narrative and performance. As narrative and performance represent enacted events available to the senses, they open themselves up to dialogue with aesthetic discourse. In particular, aesthetic discourse relates to virtue ethic discourse in at least two ways. First, within virtue ethic discourse there exists a necessary relationship between vision and ethics. As Hauerwas notes of Christian ethics, "Its first task is to help us rightly envision the world."[48] While one might argue that Hauerwas is writing metaphorically, I would argue along with ethicist Martha Nussbaum, herself citing novelist Henry James, that moral knowledge is not about propositions but perception. It is about seeing the complexity of material and social reality with both imagination and feeling.[49] The formation of virtue is the training of the individual's vision to perceive the world through the moral judgments of the community. Because of the role the senses play in this perception and judgment, they represent learned aesthetic skills. Second, because action is embodied, it is also available to the senses and thus also becomes the subject of aesthetic discourse as sensible perception. This creates the conceptual space for the framing of virtue ethics within an aesthetic framework.

Furthermore, because these events that are available to the senses represent embodied expressions of particular texts (perhaps even of particular scripts) dramatic discourse also presents itself as an

---

agent, she writes, "It would seem, then, that magnanimity in fact involves serious self-deception, inasmuch as the magnanimous person fails to remember the goods she has received from others and thus arrives at a false estimate of her own self-sufficient greatness" (*Putting on Virtue*, 42). Thus any effort to advocate for virtue ethics must make every effort to balance the community's role in moral formation, and the individual moral agent's choices which mark both the ends and means of that formation.

48 Hauerwas, *Peaceable Kingdom*, 29.

49 Nussbaum, *Love's Knowledge*, 152. Specifically, she writes that moral knowledge "is not about propositions; it is not simply intellectual grasp of particular facts; it is perception. It is seeing a complex, concrete reality in a highly lucid and richly responsive way; it is taking in what is there, with imagination and feeling."

organically fitting metaphor available to creatively describe the processes of moral formation within virtue ethics.[50] Engaging dramatic discourse then also becomes a way of providing a thick description of the aesthetic processes that are fundamental to moral formation.

CONCLUSION

Aesthetic formational processes are fundamental to human existence. They are part and parcel of existing as an embodied being in a material world. Recognizing and naming the importance of the body and the affections, people throughout history have created aesthetic texts and material culture as a means of engaging those affections and bodies. Evangelicals are no different. Evangelicals create aesthetic texts that are paradigmatic of a particular, austere disposition toward the materiality of creation. Because of their theological commitments, many Evangelicals are unable to perceive the competing sets of ongoing aesthetic moral and devotional formations in the midst of their communities as the bodies and affections of the members of those communities engage the myriad aesthetic texts and pieces of material culture that envelop them. The naming of these aesthetic processes has the aesthetic and ethical effect of articulating the persuasive power of aesthetic environments. By focusing on and naming the aesthetic moral formation that occurs, these processes may become less hidden.

50 Sam Wells does a compelling job of arguing for just this point in *Improvisation: The Drama of Christian Ethics* (Brazos, 2004).

CHAPTER 2

Evangelicals and Aesthetic Texts

> All our knowledge of the world is embodied knowledge and it is necessarily entangled in the world in which it is part. There would be no knowledge without bodies and no bodies without their constitutive relations to the world.
>
> —Mayra Rivera, *Poetics of the Flesh*

If Evangelicals are formed through their bodies and affections, then there must be Evangelical sights, sounds, and textures funding that formation. These would be the sights that wordlessly air doctrinal concerns; sounds expressing the devotion of singers in stirring melodies that carry songs to emotional heights. They would be textures weaving social and political commitments into a fabric that knits communities together around a common sense of the world and culture. Liturgical, gastronomic, familial, economic, and benevolent practices grow out of these sights, sounds, and textures. Think of paintings in church lobbies, the songs on Christian radio, shops selling books, devotional materials and knickknacks, and the films narrating a story contending for faith in the public square of the cinema. All of these and so much more instantiate the aesthetic texts that represent the Evangelical aesthetic environment. These are the sights, sounds, and textures that represent a vital part of the making of both Evangelicalism and of individual Evangelicals. And these are the sights, sounds, and textures that work to form the affections and imaginations of the Evangelicals who engage them.

Evangelicalism is surely a doctrinal, social, devotional, and political project. It is also an aesthetic project, and in order to fully understand Evangelicalism it must be understood as an aesthetic. It is an aesthetic because it encourages a particular way of seeing and perceiving. It encourages the fashioning of aesthetic texts that instantiate a particular aesthetic sense, or a particular set of aesthetic commitments if you will. In doing so, it shapes the perceptions and dispositions of Evangelicals to love and appreciate that aesthetic sense, and to perceive the world around them through the lens of that aesthetic sense. In addition, aesthetic texts, and this Evangelical aesthetic, instantiate a particular set of visions of the good life, cultivating the perceptions of that which is beautiful, good, and true.

The question of what makes an Evangelical is a much-asked question in recent national discourse, both in churches and in public conversation. However, there is no one definitive answer. Even from Evangelicalism's outset following the First and Second Great Awakenings in the American British Colonies and then later in the nascent United States in the eighteenth and nineteenth centuries, a consistent Evangelicalism has never existed. For instance, the Evangelicalism that developed in the United States grew into something different than the same movement in Britain, fostered by some of the same clergy, such as John Wesley and George Whitefield.[1] In addition, the Evangelicalism that developed in the Unites States, with all of its American idiosyncrasies, has historically carried in itself tensions that have caused it to crack, splinter, and branch out over the years. The Holiness Movement, Fundamentalism, Pentecostalism, and New Evangelicalism all represent moments where Evangelicalism has split, creating novel expressions of it.[2] Furthermore, contemporary Evangelicalism, whose origins are rooted geographically in Western

1 See Nathan O. Hatch, *The Democratization of American Christianity* (Yale University Press, 1989), 50, 143, 211–12.

2 Hatch, *Democratization of American Christianity*, 214.

Europe and North America, no longer represents a fundamentally European or North American movement. Evangelicalism now represents a worldwide movement, with more self-identifying Evangelical Christians living in the Global South (sub-Saharan Africa, the Middle East and North Africa, Latin America and most of Asia) than the Global North (Europe, North America, Japan, Australia, and New Zealand).[3] Evangelicals outside of the United States even tend to understand themselves differently than Evangelicals in the United States.

As an example, when asked, "What does it take to be a good Evangelical?" at the Third Lausanne Congress of World Evangelization in 2010, Evangelical leaders from around the globe largely agreed on three items. The first two, "following the teachings of Christ in one's personal and family life," and "working to lead others to Christ," were agreed upon with near unanimity, while "working to help the poor and needy" was agreed upon by nearly three-quarters of the respondents.[4] Notice that their responses frame Evangelicalism in terms of its actions and practices. Contrast that with the answer to the slightly different question, "What is an Evangelical?" offered by the National Association of Evangelicals, an association founded in 1942 to distinguish Evangelicals in the United States from both Fundamentalist and Progressive Christians. Drawing on historian David Bebbington's quadrilateral of Evangelical distinctives, they submit that Evangelicals are distinguished by (1) Conversionism—the belief that lives need to be transformed through a born-again experience and a lifelong process of following Jesus; (2) Biblicism—a high regard for and obedience to the Bible as the ultimate authority; (3) Activism—the expression and demonstration of the gospel in missionary and social reform efforts; and (4) Crucicentrism—a stress on the sacrifice of Jesus Christ on the cross as making possible

3 See Luis Lugo and Alan Cooperman, "Global Survey of Evangelical Protestant Leaders," Pew Research Center, June 22, 2011, https://www.pewresearch.org/religion/2011/06/22/global-survey-preface/.

4 Lugo and Cooperman, "Global Survey of Evangelical Protestant Leaders."

the redemption of humanity.[5] Notice their answers move beyond practices alone and focus also on beliefs and the experiences that should be common to all Evangelicals. Evangelicals both globally and in the United States offer slightly varied approaches as they attempt to answer similar questions. While each endeavors to answer the question in fundamentally Evangelical terms, each also reveals a bit of the distance and difference between global and American Evangelicalisms. Evangelicals, however, are not the only ones endeavoring to answer questions relating to their identity.

Journalist and historian Francis Fitzgerald in her tome on the history of Evangelicalism ultimately identifies them as those who self-identify as such, or those who are a member of a denomination that identifies themselves as such.[6] However, she also traces the growing role politics, and particularly conservative politics, has played in shaping and demarcating notions of identity among white Evangelicals in the United States.[7] Historian of religion and former president of Wake Forest University Nathan Hatch argues that from the time of their origins, particularly following the Second Great Awakening, American Evangelicals have harbored and can be identified by an anti-institutional and individualistic disposition, accompanied by a strong populist streak, which represent a set of dispositions that are actively carried over into our contemporary context.[8] Historian Kristin Kobes Du Mez frames Evangelicalism, among white Americans in particular, around its love of traditional gender roles, particularly framing Evangelicalism in terms of its strong sense of a bellicose and privileged masculinity.[9] Historian

5 See National Association of Evangelicals, "What Is an Evangelical?," National Association of Evangelicals, https://www.nae.org/what-is-an-evangelical/.

6 Francis Fitzgerald, *The Evangelicals: The Struggle to Shape America* (Simon & Schuster, 2017), 637.

7 In particular see chapters 14, 15, and 17 of Fitzgerald, *The Evangelicals*.

8 Hatch, *Democratization of American Christianity*, 5.

9 See Kristin Kobes Du Mez, *Jesus and John Wayne: How White Evangelicals Corrupted a Faith and Fractured a Nation* (Liveright Publishing Corporation, 2020).

of religion Todd Brenneman argues that white Evangelicalism in the United States can be best identified by a privileging of sentimentality as its primary defining characteristic.[10] Religion scholar John Stackhouse frames Evangelicalism as a middle or third way between conservatism and liberalism, appropriating traditions from across Christian denominations and practices to suit the doctrinal and devotional commitments particular communities believe to be the most important expressions of Christianity as they see them.[11] Theologian Amos Yong frames American Evangelicals alongside their global counterparts and argues that Evangelicalism, understood broadly, must always understand itself as a fundamentally enculturated, contextual, and vernacular theology and community in order for it to make sense both to itself and to the world in which it is embedded.[12] These approaches, of course, represent less than a drop in the proverbial bucket of Evangelical scholarship. All that being said, identifying Evangelicals as those who self-identify as such, or who are members of denominations that identify as Evangelical, provides both the most reasonable and most generous set of delineations for the project at hand. The visual, aural, and embodied components that accompany those self-identifications provide the most complete representation of Evangelicalism. In the end, its aesthetic texts will prove as helpful in identifying Evangelicals as any doctrine or devotional practice.

10 See Todd Brenneman, *Homespun Gospel: The Triumph of Sentimentality in Contemporary American Evangelicalism* (Oxford University Press, 2014).

11 John G. Stackhouse Jr., *Evangelicalism: A Very Short Introduction* (Oxford University Press, 2022), 24.

12 See Amos Yong, *The Future of Evangelical Theology: Soundings from the Asian American Diaspora* (IVP Academic, 2014). He goes on to recognize the multitude of opportunities available to Asian American Evangelicals, and particularly Asian American Pentecostal Evangelicals, to contribute to the construction of that contextualized theology alongside and in the midst of the broader set of (white) Evangelical institutions in the United States.

THE AESTHETIC SHAPES OF EVANGELICALISM

To begin to assess and frame an Evangelical aesthetic, look to the films, music, novels, self-help books, knickknacks, visual art, and the various other pieces of material culture created, manufactured, or sold by and for the benefit of Evangelicals. Church historian Todd Brenneman does just that in his book *Homespun Gospel: The Triumph of Sentimentality in Contemporary American Evangelicalism.* In arguing that sentimentality represents a key to interpreting and understanding modern white Evangelicalism, he also recognizes the fundamentally aesthetic nature of his argument: "They [Evangelicals] live in an aesthetic world where emotion is the currency to interact not only with other human beings but also with God. They produce commodities that enable themselves to 'feel as though it expresses what is common among them' without recognizing the differences."[13] He goes on to note, "Evangelicals are replicating a culture of emotionality—particularly sentimental emotionality—with almost every book or album they produce, implanting sentimentality in the lived experience of consumers who read the book, listen to the music, or watch the video."[14] The material culture and aesthetic texts produced and consumed by Evangelicals instantiate particular ways of seeing, perceiving, and being in the world that are learned through their bodies. This is because Evangelicals learn what it means to be an Evangelical through their bodies.

With a definition of aesthetic that focuses on embodied, sensible perception, the aesthetic texts and pieces of material culture that are produced for the benefit of Evangelicals do their formational work in them. In doing so they are engaging their bodies and emotions for the purposes of shaping their perceptions of the physical, cultural, and political landscapes. Aesthetic texts work to form the Evangelical's tastes and preferences in separating the kinds and types of music, movies, and books they should like from the ones they should reject.

---

13 Brenneman, *Homespun Gospel*, 13.

14 Brenneman, *Homespun Gospel*, 14.

Understanding the process by which this formation occurs is key to understanding Evangelicalism as an aesthetic.

Twentieth-century French sociologist Pierre Bourdieu's account of the social function of taste, which is also the social function of the aesthetic, offers useful insight, naming the processes that fund this type of formation. In his book *Distinction: A Social Critique of the Judgement of Taste*, Bourdieu wants to frame the development of aesthetic judgment and taste as directly rooted in the body.[15] In particular Bourdieu connects the origins of aesthetic taste to the development of one's food preferences.[16] Beginning from that point he branches out to account for the interplay of cultural, social, and economic forces in the development of matters of taste.[17]

---

15 Here Bourdieu is playing in the waters of eighteenth-century German philosopher Immanuel Kant's aesthetics. Kant's approach to aesthetics endeavors to describe the relationship between beauty and the senses in essentially empirical terms. Kant argues that beauty is a universal quality that is agreed upon by all, but is only experienced subjectively (Immanuel Kant, *Critique of Judgment*, ed. Nicholas Walker, trans. James Creed Meredith [Oxford University Press, 2007], 48–51). However, for Kant, beauty is not a formal quality of the beautiful object itself. Thus the pleasure one receives in the presence of beauty, regardless of whether the object that inspires that pleasure is cultural or natural, is not a pleasure rooted in the senses. This pleasure then can be said to be disinterested; that is, it is a pleasure interested in a beauty that is not intrinsic to the beautiful object, and therefore not directly available to the senses (54). It is a pleasure that is disinterested in a beautiful object's physical particulars. The individual's experience of aesthetic pleasure is achieved as one contemplates the object's aesthetic qualities. Through the practice of this process, the individual develops the taste to discern beauty and thus encounter the sublime. Bourdieu simultaneously critiques the limited role the body plays in Kant's aesthetic while embracing the social role of aesthetic taste. Bourdieu's work can also be seen as an attempt to describe sociologically the manner in which Kant's notion of the aesthetic is formed and operates in individuals and the social structures that surround them.

16 Bourdieu, *Distinction*, 1.

17 I must acknowledge here that Bourdieu's analysis is done specifically in the context of a formally stratified French culture. There are bound to be disparities when attempting to analogously relate his analysis to American and Evangelical American contexts, and of course to non-Eurocentric contexts; however I argue that the specificity of his cultural and aesthetic analysis can yield insights into aesthetic formation that can dialogue across cultural

Bourdieu's construction of taste on the foundation of the physical consumption and tasting of food means that his cultural and social approach to the aesthetic is built on the body and the senses. But Bourdieu moves beyond food, arguing that an individual's aesthetic preferences are also shaped through one's physical interaction with and relationship to other sensory (aesthetic) objects as well. This means that the individual's aesthetic preferences have also been shaped by their interactions with items such as home furnishings, silverware, cookery, wall adornments, automobiles, recreation and sports equipment, smartphones, computers, television, and the videos and music that are played on those phones, computers, and televisions. An individual's aesthetic preferences for Bourdieu are shaped by the entirety of the materiality in which they are embedded. The actions, practices, and even rituals associated with these objects, repeated over days, months, and years, form what Bourdieu calls the *habitus*, which is a set of dispositions formed by these repeated actions and practices.

These repeated actions and practices over time form the individual's affections and the imagination; the things we love, and the conceptual framework through which we perceive the world.[18] Stated idiomatically we might say that the habitus is caught not taught.

In addition, because the relationship to material culture is fundamentally related to the quality of that material culture (envision the difference in quality and amenities between a car built by an economy auto manufacturer and a car built by a luxury auto manufacturer), aesthetic preferences become a means to assert one's social position.[19]

---

differences because of his emphasis on the role played by the senses and the body in that formation. While the notion of and relationship to the human body will surely differ from culture to culture, I argue that the body's role in the formation of the affections and perception remains a constant within the human experience. As such I argue that Bourdieu's insights might prove useful for attempting to dialogue, even across those cultural barriers.

18 Because of this, Bourdieu notes that the schemes of the habitus "function below the level of consciousness and language, beyond the reach of introspective scrutiny or control by the will" (*Distinction*, 466.)

19 Bourdieu, *Distinction*, 57.

The entirety of this embodied and social relationship to cultural and aesthetic objects is what Bourdieu frames as taste.[20] This is why for Bourdieu taste is fundamentally shaped by the material culture and the aesthetic texts an individual and community see, hear, touch, taste, and feel.[21] Thus, particular dispositions toward specific pieces of material culture will depend on the taste that is formed through the individual's interactions with those pieces of material culture that have most fundamentally formed that person's and the community's

---

20 Bourdieu argues that taste is "the propensity and capacity to appropriate (materially or symbolically) a given class of classified, classifying objects or practices" (173). Articulating the implications of this understanding, Bourdieu writes, "Taste is the practical operator of the transmutation of things into distinct and distinctive signs" (174). Thus within this framework, every appropriation of an aesthetic or cultural object constitutes a relation of distinction. (227).

21 Important to understanding Bourdieu's physical, social, aesthetic framework here is its simultaneous relationship to economics. Bourdieu employs an economic framework for understanding the relationship between the social, aesthetic, economic, cultural, and educational spheres. He argues that each should be understood as different types of capital. Within his construct one does not simply climb a social ladder for example, one exchanges or converts educational capital into social, cultural, or economic capital (125). Thus a person's habitus is formed within this framework of competing capitals. The habitus of an individual raised in the context of large pools of economic and social capital is going to be formed and form that individual differently than the habitus of an individual raised in the context of moderate pools of the same capital. This is largely because of the type and quality of the material objects each individual's practices are shaped by and around. Thus Bourdieu can write, "Every material inheritance is, strictly speaking, also a cultural inheritance. Family heirlooms not only bear material witness to the age and continuity of the lineage and so consecrate its social identity. . . . They also contribute in a practical way to its spiritual reproduction." (76). Bourdieu argues that an individual's economic and thus social capital are the most significant variables that contribute to that individual's cultural and aesthetic capital, and ultimately his or her aesthetic disposition (53). Bourdieu does acknowledge that cultural and aesthetic capital can be gained through educational capital; however he also argues that the one who gains that capital in that manner is less native to that environment than the one whose habitus was formed as a child in the context of extended cultural capital (66).

affections; that is those pieces of material culture that are themselves most beloved (perhaps even held most sacred) by the community.[22]

A wonderful example of this simultaneously aesthetic and social process is offered by historian Lawrence W. Levine. He traces the cultural and social roles performed by the plays of William Shakespeare in the United States beginning in the early nineteenth century through the middle of the twentieth century. In doing so he offers a narrative snapshot of these aesthetic processes that form taste, perceptions, and dispositions. Levine notes that in the early nineteenth century the American theater was a largely egalitarian institution. It was a space where a cross-section of socioeconomic groups would not only sit alongside one another but would interact with one another.[23] As the century progressed these socially open practices began to wane, and by the end of the nineteenth century the theater physically instantiated social distinctions through the physical separation of socioeconomic groups. As these material distinctions grew the physical distance that created these distinctions would then become embedded in cultural practices and imaginations.

As the United States approached the turn of the twentieth century, the theater came to represent the enforcement of aesthetic, cultural, and ultimately social and economic distinctions. The construction of physical representations of distinction (the creation of pits and galleries, and ultimately different theaters) represents the material and institutional expression of those differences in taste. Thus, the story

22 A good example of this type of dispositional formation might be the manner in which music forms an individual and community's affections. There are many who have grown up listening to contemporary Christian Music (CCM), or who actively listen to modern worship music, whose dispositions toward music, theology, liturgy, and social structures have been fundamentally shaped through these sets of aesthetic texts. Pete Ward offers an insightful account of these processes. See Pete Ward, "Affective Alliance or Circuits of Power: The Production and Consumption of Contemporary Charismatic Worship in Britain," *International Journal of Practical Theology* 9, no. 1 (2005): 25–39, at 29, 30.

23 Lawrence W. Levine, *Highbrow/Lowbrow: The Emergence of Cultural Hierarchy in America* (Harvard University Press, 1988), 57.

Levine tells as it relates to the changing social and cultural perceptions of Shakespeare's plays in the nineteenth and early twentieth centuries in America frames Bourdieu's argument that the formation of taste is fundamentally embedded in the web of material culture. As that material culture adjusts to reflect the aesthetic commitments and the habitus of its creators, it also forms individual and community perceptions of cultural, aesthetic, and social norms, thus operating to reshape other's affections, and ultimately their habitus.

If true, this aesthetic formation of taste also means that the taste formed among those embedded in more popular expressions of material culture also embody the cultural, aesthetic, and social commitments instantiated in those expressions. For Bourdieu, the process by which taste, affections, and the habitus are formed is the same regardless of the quality and type of the material culture it is being formed in relation to. Within this framework, there is no escape from the formational influence of material culture.

Within an Evangelical context, the aesthetic texts and the material culture that Evangelicals create, produce, consume, share, and love are also working to shape their taste. These aesthetic texts include the Evangelical films, music, novels, self-help books, knickknacks, and visual art that constitute significant portions of the Evangelical aesthetic environment. They work to form imaginations, perceptions, and dispositions in ways similar to the changing aesthetic commitments the grew alongside the staging Shakespeare's plays in the United States led to the construction of separate spaces for aesthetic and social classes that grew out of those commitments. Evangelicals' aesthetic texts provide similar notions of aesthetic and cultural identity. These run parallel to and overlap with non-Evangelical aesthetic texts and culture, using the same movie theaters for films, bookstores for books, concert halls for comedy shows, and arenas for concerts, but they still represent separate spaces for a separated Evangelical community. That Evangelical environment alongside the social constructs that accompany those texts are helping to shape notions of the type and character of aesthetic texts that are preferred and the type that earn Evangelical antipathy. They are fundamental to forming Evangelical aesthetic dispositions, and ultimately their habitus, their way of being in the world. The implications of this formation however do not stop here. If material culture works to form the affections and imaginations of those who engage it, then it simultaneously accomplishes the formation of notions of the good life and the formation of the moral imagination for Evangelicals.

EVANGELICALISM AS THE GOOD LIFE

To account for the role taste and the aesthetic play in the formation of notions of the good life, eighteenth-century Scottish philosopher, ethicist, and economist Adam Smith is particularly helpful because his approach to understanding the formation of virtue and morality is simultaneously aesthetic and social. For him, virtue and morality are formed through sensual and social experience, particularly focused on the social power of sight and imagination. Specifically, he argues that moral formation should be framed by the notion of sympathy. As a foundational principle, Smith writes, "As we have no immediate experience of what other men feel, we can form no idea of the manner in which they are affected, but by conceiving what we ourselves should feel in the like situation."[24] Thus Smith understands sympathy as rooted in the imagination.[25] As an example Smith cites the imagined pain one feels when they witness someone else experience a significant blow or injury.[26]

This reflexive shrinking back is a product of an embodied imagination. One who has experienced the pain of a similar, even if less severe, injury intuitively remembers the pain associated with it. Imagining that pain anew, he moves instinctually to protect himself

---

24 Adam Smith, *Theory of Moral Sentiments*, 1 (I.I.2).

25 Here Smith writes, "We sometimes feel for another, a passion of which he himself seems to be altogether incapable; because, when we put ourselves in his case, that passion arises in our breast from the imagination (*Theory of Moral Sentiments*, 4 [I.I.10]).

26 Smith, *Theory of Moral Sentiments*, 20 (I.II.7).

from the imagined blow.[27] Smith argues that this viscerally sympathetic relationship to the other is the universal root of human systems of morality and ethics.[28]

Smith argues, building on his notion of sympathy, that when people begin to form their own moral framework, they judge their own actions and practices as if they were judging another's.[29]

For Smith, ethical action and practices, and indeed morality, are built upon the individual's ability to imagine the manner in which a virtuous person, as they understand that concept, would judge his or her actions. This imagining of the judgment of the other is built around the individual's sense of the type of acts that might be praised and condemned.[30] This imagination of course is itself

27 On a side note, I argue that this protective impulse is part of the reason for the niche popularity of the horror and slasher film genres. The pleasure associated with viewing them is rooted in the viscerally imagined, embodied experiences associated with the narrative and visual construction of the film, which generally emphasizes physical vulnerability and pain, or at least the threat of pain.

28 Here we must acknowledge that the universality of Smith's claims reflect the thought processes endemic to his Enlightenment roots. His claims are more properly framed within the particularity of a Western European framework, and perhaps even more properly within the framework of the sociality and manners among eighteenth-century Scottish and English gentry with which he was familiar. Acknowledging Smith's limitations, I believe he is still useful in the context of my argument. What is particularly useful to the argument I am making is Smith's assertion that ethics and morality are formed in relation to bodily perception and the aesthetic.

29 Thus Smith writes, "The principle by which we naturally approve or disapprove of our own conduct, seems to be altogether the same with that by which we exercise the like judgments concerning the conduct of other people. We either approve or disapprove of the conduct of another man according as we feel that, when we bring his case home to ourselves, we either can or cannot entirely sympathize with the sentiments and motives which directed it. And, in the same manner, we either approve or disapprove of our own conduct, according as we feel that, when we place ourselves in the situation of another man, and view it, as it were, with his eyes and from his station, we either can or cannot entirely enter into and sympathize with the sentiments and motives which influenced it" (*Theory of Moral Sentiments*, 93 [III.I.2]).

30 Smith, *Theory of Moral Sentiments*, 134 (III.I.95). Smith frames these as approbation and censure.

built on the experiences of the body as it encounters and internalizes the aesthetic and ethical framework of the social body. This is because sight is a fundamentally embodied act that should not be isolated from the other senses and is best understood as an act that is socially constructed.[31] Sight then works to integrate the body of the individual and the body of the group.[32] David Morgan employs the aesthetic notion of the gaze, the manner in which one learns to perceive the world, to parse out the ways in which one's individual body is integrated into the social body.[33] With the gaze comes the knowledge, or at least the intuition, that one is always in another's field of vision and is thus constantly subject to the gaze of both the individual bodies of others and the larger social body.

Morgan argues that this shared sight and these shared ways of seeing shape individual and social bodies, particularly as they take part in communities organized around shared forms of intuition, imagination, and bodily practices as they are in religious communities.[34] Thus the gaze "is a practice (conscious or unconscious) which structures social relations, self-concept, and the experience of the

---

31 See Morgan, *The Embodied Eye*, xvii. I must acknowledge here that Morgan is principally interested in people's relationships to material objects and the manner in which the practices of individuals and religious communities are shaped by them, particularly as they are sensed visually. Morgan has no intent of directly linking his work to conversations regarding ethics. However, I argue that in light of Smith's aesthetic and social approach to ethics, Morgan's scholarship becomes useful in describing the processes that go unarticulated in Smith's work. In addition, I will be making the case in a later chapter that practices themselves (framed dramatically) are best understood as innately aesthetic. One's actions are always subject to the gaze and thus are not only shaped by the gaze of others but are simultaneously and constantly shaping the practices and imagination of other individuals and the collective imagination of the social body. I argue that this is at least implicit in the larger argument that Smith is making.

32 Morgan, *The Embodied Eye*, 14.

33 We saw last chapter that in describing the gaze he argued, "Seeing is the development of a visual routine that organizes the visual field, enacting within its structures, desire, fear, companionship or authority that shapes visual experience" (Morgan, *The Embodied Eye*, 55).

34 Morgan, *The Embodied Eye*, 6.

sacred."[35] The gaze then is an unremitting force that shapes the individual's imagination and perception. Because the gaze operates through social processes, structuring social relations, it also works to organize social power structures.[36]

Smith and Morgan frame their arguments in terms of the social forces at work in aesthetic processes. Morgan then expands on Smith's ethical approach that endeavors to account for the role the aesthetic and social play in the shaping of both practical and theoretical virtue. Morgan is also helpful in that he exposes these aesthetic and social processes at work as they are instantiated in material objects and the practices associated with visual culture.[37] If this aesthetic and social understanding of formation represents an accurate depiction of human formation, then material representations of a particular community's gaze, material culture, and aesthetic texts (specifically here the Evangelical community) exert an aesthetic and social force that shape the viewer's affections and imagination. To shape an individual and community's affections and imagination is to eventually shape their concept of the good and the good life. Thus, these aesthetic texts and pieces of material culture work to express and reinforce the individual's sense of virtue and his sense of the community while simultaneously working to form the community's sense of morality and their moral imagination.[38]

---

35 Morgan, *The Embodied Eye*, 67, 68. The gaze here is framed by Morgan as the visual field or way of seeing.

36 Morgan, *The Embodied Eye*, 70.

37 We must note that Smith, in writing of moral formation, is not arguing for a principled approach to ethics in that he is not attempting to articulate universal moral principles (though he is doing his Enlightenment best to articulate universal formational principles). In doing so, Smith is trying to articulate the processes that influence and even govern the formation of individual virtue and cultural morality. Thus Smith cannot be employed to argue for the morality or immorality of particular pieces of material culture.

38 This will be picked up at a greater depth in the next chapter, particularly in conversation with Stanley Hauerwas's understanding of the power of narrative to shape virtue.

Employing Bourdieu's nomenclature, the forces operating to form this sense of morality and subsequent moral formation are a part of the formation of the individual's habitus. Additionally, because of Smith's emphasis on the affective imagination, that is engaging the imagination to judge both how certain acts would make others feel, and the manner in which those actions would be praised or condemned by the community at large, material culture and aesthetic texts can be understood to exert a particularly powerful influence over the imagination, and moral imagination, because of its direct appeal to the affections through the body. Thus, read through this combined Smith/Morgan framework, we can see the manner in which Evangelical material culture and aesthetic texts can affectively shape Evangelical moral imaginations. More importantly to the argument at hand, we can assert that they form imaginations as they relate to notions of both the good and the good life, for better or for worse.

EVANGELICALISM AND THE CULTIVATION OF PERCEPTION

"For better or for worse," because what has been described thus far are simply the processes by which the formation of one's affections, perception, and dispositions occur. The content of the texts or the trajectory of the formation have yet to be addressed. There is formational importance in both the content of the aesthetic texts and material culture that are fundamental to formation and the aesthetic manner in which they are embedded and instantiated. These aesthetic texts are fundamental not only to the formation of Evangelical affections, perceptions, and dispositions, but that because of the manner in which they shape each of these, they are fundamental to the formation of the Evangelical notions of the good life and of the notion of the good itself. Furthermore, in light of the association of beauty, goodness, and truth from classical Greek antiquity, these Evangelical aesthetic texts also work to form the perception of what constitutes the beautiful and the true as well.

The recovery of the notions of beauty, goodness, and truth (known colloquially as the transcendentals) in contemporary discourse, and particularly in theological discourse, can be at least partially traced to twentieth-century Swiss Catholic theologian Hans Urs von Balthasar, whose fifteen-volume theological magnus opus is divided into three sections: Theological Aesthetics, Theo-drama, and Theo-logic (beauty, goodness and truth). His work represents his endeavor to reclaim the notion of beauty for the purposes of theology, and place that notion into a necessarily and equally proportional relationship with goodness and truth. Near the beginning of his initial volume in this project he writes, "Our situation today shows that beauty demands for itself at least as much courage and decision as do truth and goodness, and she will not allow herself to be separated and banned from her two sisters without taking them along with herself in an act of mysterious vengeance. We can be sure that whoever sneers at her name as if she were the ornament of a bourgeois past—whether he admits it or not—can no longer pray and soon will no longer be able to love."[39] For von Balthasar to shape one's perception of the beautiful is to shape one's perception of the good (the actions that reveal that beauty), which is to simultaneously shape one's notion of what is true. Put another way, to shape one's notion of the good (in our instance by aesthetic means) is also to shape one's perception of what qualifies as lovely and attractive and what material representations and what practices associated with those materials best represent what is true. This means that the aesthetic formation that is cultivated in the individual and their community will share a direct relationship with the proportions of the beautiful, the good, and the true that is instantiated in the aesthetic texts that they come to love. The trajectory of that formation is then also in direct relation

39 Hans Urs von Balthasar, *The Glory of the Lord: A Theological Aesthetics*, vol. 1, *Seeing the Form*, trans. Erasmo Leiva-Merkakis (Ignatius Press, 1982), 18. He later notes, "The fundamental principle of a theological aesthetics . . . is the fact that, just as this revelation is absolute truth and goodness, so also it is absolute beauty" (607).

with the manner in which the aesthetic texts engaged by the community faithfully represent what is beautiful, good, and true.[40]

American theologian Willie James Jennings in his book *The Christian Imagination: Theology and the Origins of Race* offers a masterful glimpse into what it looks like for a community's and culture's moral imagination to be formed for the worse formed by centuries aesthetic texts, practices, and gazes that institute a regime that deeply distorts beauty, goodness, and truth. At the heart of Jennings's project is an argument that the Western racial imagination represents an aesthetic disposition (a habitus), formed by aesthetic means, which finds its roots in a Christian theological discourse that is committed to a colonial manner of perceiving the materiality of creation and culture, an aesthetic that correlates an individual's social and economic value to a conceptual framework attached the shade of his skin. As such, Jennings endeavors to tell the story of the processes that formed "Christianity's diseased social imagination."[41] Jennings argues that this colonial configuration of bodies and space is in fact a social, economic, and theological reconfiguration of creation for the purposes of serving the colonial project and represents a reconfiguration that continues to endure. As such this reconfiguration signifies an erasure of identities that are rooted in a particular place.[42] Jennings documents and describes in disturbing detail the social and moral consequences of the aesthetic reconfiguration of a community and

---

40 For von Balthasar the proportions of the truth were directly rooted in the beauty and glory revealed through the self-gifting love of God enacting the good through the life, death, and resurrection of Jesus. Von Balthasar writes, "The *Aesthetics* has already uncovered the glory and hence the 'beauty' of God's action, his Covenant, the fulfillment of his covenant righteousness and his judgment as a function of this fulfillment. But in doing so it has also revealed the 'goodness' of God's totally free love, without which his glory would not be beautiful or his word true" (Hans Urs von Balthasar, *Theo-Drama: Theological Dramatic Theory*, vol. 1, *Prolegomena*, trans. Graham Harrison [Ignatius Press, 1988], 18, 19)

41 Willie James Jennings, *The Christian Imagination: Theology and the Origins of Race* (Yale University Press, 2010), 9.

42 Jennings, *The Christian Imagination*, 40.

culture's sense of social perception, and subsequently its vision of the good and the good life, a process that fundamentally reshaped both white and black bodies. These represent aesthetic processes that have formed and continue to form the perceptions, imaginations and practices, as they relate to both Black and white bodies, not just in the West or in the United States, but around the world.

This, of course, is why both the ideas that are instantiated in the aesthetic and the manner in which those ideas are instantiated are important. Human imaginations are constantly and consistently being formed by that which aesthetic texts and material culture express and the way they express it. Jennings notes for us the manner in which these aesthetic processes have formed our cultural and social notions of race; however, within the aesthetic framework for which I am arguing, these aesthetic processes are constantly and relentlessly forming human perception and imaginations in every way imaginable, and in many ways we cannot imagine and fail to perceive.

CONCLUSION

The aesthetic texts created and consumed by Evangelicals are not different. They instantiate Evangelicals' aesthetic and theological commitments in ways that help to form the manner in which Evangelicals perceive the world. They instantiate visual, audio, and conceptual representations of that which they believe best represents the true, the beautiful, and the good. In doing so, they hope to recreate the perception of the good, beautiful, and true in those that engage those aesthetic texts. When Evangelicals attend Evangelical concerts or movies; when they purchase Evangelical books and knicknacks; when they worship and fellowship together, they partake together in common visions of these notions of the good, beautiful, and true. They imbibe them and embody them. They grow to love and then enact the visions of the good life that are embedded in these aesthetic texts. They participate in the cultivation of practices that recreate these visions of these beautiful, good, and true proportions.

Scholars attempting to define Evangelicalism identified many of its qualities, such as American Evangelicalism's affinity with conservative politics; its anti-institutional and populist dispositions; its affinity for traditional gender roles; its privileging of sentimentality; its affinity for appropriating theological and social traditions; and its fundamentally enculturated nature. This of course does not represent an exhaustive description of the characteristics that constitute Evangelicalism; however, if this description accurately represents a part of what makes Evangelicalism what it is, then the Evangelical aesthetic represents the aesthetic texts and material culture that cultivate these characteristics. They are the texts that frame these dispositions and the practices associated with them as the good life, and thus as beautiful and true.

CHAPTER 3

Moral Formation and the Aesthetics of Virtue

> Your love or desire—aimed at a vision of the good life that shapes how you see the world while also moving and motivating you—is operative on a largely nonconscious level. Your love is a kind of automaticity. That's why we need to be aware of how it is acquired.
>
> —James K. A. Smith, *You Are What You Love: The Spiritual Power of Habit*

People engage in activities they love. They volunteer at community organizations and churches. They attend sporting events, concerts, and theater performances. They watch thirty-second videos on tiny screens, thirty-minute television shows on medium-sized screens, and two-hour movies on large screens. They exercise, cook, play with their pets, and nap in their homes. They meet friends for drinks, food, and coffee in local eateries and bars. (In short people engage the aesthetic texts such as television, movies, and music, material culture such a books, wall art, and knickknacks, and the practices that they love.) Evangelicals are no different. However, in addition to their engagement with the aesthetic texts of popular culture, and Evangelical popular culture, they gather weekly to be formed by aesthetic means. They gather to have their affections, dispositions, and practices formed by the songs, sermons, communion, and fellowship that make up their weekly church services. They return week by week to be formed by the church's liturgies. In each of these instances the people interacting with these movies, music, books, knickknacks, and liturgies are engaging each by means of their bodies and thus their senses, meaning each falls within the realm or the aesthetic. In each of these instances, these aesthetic texts are not only expressions of the imaginations and dispositions of those who created these texts. As expressions of their creators' affections and imaginations they also work to form the affections, imaginations, and dispositions of those who repeatedly engage them. As each aesthetic text instantiates their creator's visions of the good life, they can also come to form the reader's, viewer's, or audience's practices as well.

Because of the way virtue ethics understands the formational power of the ends or aims one loves or is endeavoring to achieve, virtue ethic discourse provides a useful means of framing the processes facilitating a person's moral formation by these aesthetic processes. In addition, the formation envisioned in virtue ethic discourse springs from narrative and performance, which represent the aesthetic and dramatic processes which fund moral formation. This is because narrative and performance employ both aesthetic and dramatic means to form ethical dispositions.

VIRTUE ETHICS AND THE ELEMENTS OF DRAMA

Narrative

Narrative shapes the imaginations and dispositions of its participants through their gazes and bodies. If one is growing from the person they are at the moment into the person they could or perhaps should be, that person is living a story.[1] Though they may not find themselves on the epic hero's journey, they are always changing, for both better

---

1 See Kotva, *Christian Case for Virtue Ethics*, 17; Kotva notes that virtue ethics "deals with the transition from who we are to who we could be" (17).

and perhaps for worse. Narrative provides a framework for a person to attribute meaning to the growth and change of their moral agency. Narrative helps one make sense of events and experience through the articulation of the elements that make up narrative, such as motivation, theme, setting, and plot. This self-narration allows the person to attempt to fit their story, as they understand it, into the larger narratives of their community or culture.

Advocates of virtue ethics argue that the inclination to organize our own experiences into a cogent narrative is a fundamentally human quality. To paraphrase Alisdair MacIntyre, to be a human animal is to be a narrative animal.[2] There is something fundamentally human about finding narrative appealing, enjoyable, illuminating, and ultimately necessary. It also contains the power to affect one's imagination and practice.

Philosopher and ethicist Martha Nussbaum addresses similar concerns in *Love's Knowledge*, her collection of essays on philosophy, literature, and ethics. She argues that the complexities endemic to modernity, and to the social, political, cultural, and religious nature of interpersonal reality, requires a perceptive apparatus trained to properly read these complexities.[3] Relying on novelist Henry James she argues that narrative, particularly in the form of stories and novels, "cultivate our ability to see and care for particulars, not as representatives of a law, but as what they themselves are: to respond vigorously with senses and emotion before the new; to care deeply about chance happenings in the world, rather than fortify ourselves against them; to wait for the outcome and to be bewildered—to wait and float and be actively passive."[4] For Nussbaum, the narrative form itself allows for this more passive reception of the ideas it embodies,

2 See MacIntyre, *After Virtue*, 216.

3 We had quoted her previously, arguing, "Moral knowledge, James suggests, is not simply intellectual grasp of propositions; it is not even simply intellectual grasp of particular facts; it is perception. It is seeing a complex, concrete reality in a highly lucid and richly responsive way; it is taking in what is there, with imagination and feeling" (*Love's Knowledge*, 152).

4 Nussbaum, *Love's Knowledge*, 184.

relative to strictly rational or propositional language, because its reception is as affective as it is rational. She argues that narrative accomplishes this because when it is at its best, particularly when its descriptions of the world are nuanced, dense, concrete, and subtle, it achieves a thick yet affective account of the world that is unattainable through propositional language alone.[5] Thus she might argue that narrative is most effective when it is most poetic.

Fellow James disciple Flannery O'Connor provides a similar description of this process, though through the eyes of a novelist. She argues, engaging James's categories, that the author's ability to clearly render the "felt life" of the world he is creating, that is the degree to which the narrative world rings true to natural and human complexities as we experience them, is dependent upon the author's own perceptive apparatus.[6] The more developed the novelist's sense of vision, the more detail, nuance, and subtlety she can embody in her stories.[7] Additionally she recognizes that a story, regardless of length, represents an irreducible unit of meaning:

> A story is a way to say something that can't be said any other way, and it takes every word in the story to say what the meaning is. You tell a story because a statement would be inadequate. When anybody asks what the story is about, the only proper thing is to tell him to read the story. The meaning of fiction is not abstract meaning but experienced meaning, and the purpose of making statements about the meaning of a story is only to help you to experience that meaning more fully.[8]

---

5 Nussbaum, *Love's Knowledge*, 5. If this is the case, academics must acknowledge that novelists and poets are far more adept at accomplishing that which I am attempting to accomplish here. While academics may analyze these narratives employing propositional language, the novelist and poet can touch and describe those same truths in a far more holistic and affective manner.

6 Flannery O'Connor, *Mystery and Manners: Occasional Prose*, ed. Sally Fitzgerald and Robert Fitzgerald (Farrar, Straus & Giroux, 1969), 67, 146.

7 O'Connor goes further to argue that his moral sense will be directly connected to their sense of vision, writing, "in the greatest depth of vision, moral judgment will be implicit" (*Mystery and Manners*, 30).

8 O'Connor, *Mystery and Manners*, 96.

A narrative's meaning can be found in a manner that is only accomplished through the narrative form, and through that form it embodies the author's sense of moral vision, and articulates it in a manner that is imbibed affectively by the reader or hearer.[9] In this way, narrative's method of accomplishing the articulation of meaning differs from discourse that privileges the rational and propositional. Narrative explicitly carves out space for the interpretive role of affect alongside the interpretive role played by reason. The narrative form then gives a formal voice to the human impulse toward meaning making, while simultaneously creating space to process that meaning both rationally and affectively. This does not mean there is a duality between affect and reason or between narrative and propositional forms of discourse. Affect and reason represent contrasting means of knowledge formation within an epistemological continuum, meaning that most discourse exists in the shades between the affective and the rational.[10]

With this approach to narrative, fiction and nonfiction should not be considered separately since I am arguing for an aesthetic understanding of narrative. The descriptions provided by Nussbaum and O'Connor relating to how narratives operate on a person applies to both fictional and non-fictional narrative. Put simply, both fictional and nonfictional narratives affect the subject in the same manner. For example, documentary films can produce as affective an experience as dramatic or comedic films. Here the narrative form is the key, not the content of the narrative. Regardless of the form the narrative takes (here distinguished between fiction and nonfiction), the experience

9 Nussbaum argues the affective power of story and narrative along with its ability to embody and articulate moral truth is rooted in its form and style. Put in another way, how a story goes about the work of making meaning is as, if not more important, than the particulars of what it means—or perhaps better, any notion of inherent meaning. Form and style are inseparable.

10 I can sense a potential objection here, as some might argue that I am conflating the affective power of fictional narratives (which have been the subject of our focus on narrative thus far) with what might be called the rationality of nonfiction narratives. The question of whether they should be considered separately or at the least be subject to differing methodologies comes to the fore.

of it in the subject always contains an affective and a subsequently formative component.[11] In that vein, a person's affective disposition and the manner in which they perceive the events that occur in the world around them on local, regional, national, and international stages is shaped by the narratives they engage and develop an affection for, and the manner in which these narratives frame and describe these worlds. This may be why those that regularly watch CNN and MSNBC perceive the world differently from those who regularly watch Fox News and Newsmax. If viewed through this lens, one can argue that their differences are as aesthetic as they are ideological; or perhaps better, one's ideological bents and dispositions are first shaped by aesthetic means.

Another example of the affective power of narrative in both fiction and nonfiction (and perhaps even as the two intermingle) is provided by Todd Brenneman and his study of Evangelical sentimentality particularly as exemplified in the writing of Max Lucado. Brenneman notes that narrativity is the primary tool employed by Lucado to enrich and develop his reader's religious and spiritual devotion. Lucado interlaces fictional narratives of his own creation with nonfictional and biblical narratives to accomplish these ends. He employs narrative methodology for two reasons. First, this approach functions to supplement his authority. Brenneman notes, "The conflation of these self-centered experiences—the relationship between God and the believer integrated with the relationship of Lucado and the reader—is meant to lead the reader to take the words and ideas

11 Aristotle's *Poetics* briefly consider similar questions, parsing out the relative importance of tragedy, comedy, epic, poetry, music, and history: "The distinction between historian and poet is not in the one writing prose and the other verse—you might put the work of Herodotus into verse, and in this, that the one describes the thing that has been, and the other a kind of thing that might be. Hence poetry is something more philosophic and of graver import than history, since its statements are of the nature rather of universals, whereas those of history are singulars." (Aristotle, *Aristotle's Poetics*, trans. George Whalley, John Baxter, and Patrick Atherton Montreal [McGill-Queen's University Press, 1997], IX.) Here he frames each as a narrative that embodies its own method of affect.

Lucado offers as if they were the words of God."[12] Second, because of the affectivity inherent to narrative, Lucado can interlace different types of narrative to accomplish his intended devotional ends. Lucado understands the power of the narrative form, and through interlacing his accounts of fictional and nonfictional events with biblical narratives he creates an affective means of bolstering his reader's Christian devotion.

The power of narrative lies not in its content, but in its form. Within the virtue ethic framework narrative operates to form the moral agent's affections and dispositions. These affections and dispositions then become enacted, which leads to narrative's formative companion: performance.

Performance

Narrative may shape the desires of the moral agent, but ethical discourse is less concerned about desire than it is about action. Sam Wells notes that if the subject of ethics is the formation of virtue then narrative alone cannot account for this formation. Virtue ethic discourse attempts to account for the processes that form an agent's moral habits. To account for the formation of the moral agent's habits and actions, one must look to performance. Once performance is introduced to the conversation, drama becomes the aesthetic lens necessary to account for that formation.[13] It becomes the aesthetic

12 Todd Brenneman, "Traveling Light: Max Lucado and the Power of Sentimentality in American Evangelicalism" (PhD diss., The Florida State University, 2009), 18. Lucado of course is not the first to employ these means to bolster the appearance of authority. Danté employed similar methods in his *Commedia*, and for similar reasons, to encourage and deepen the devotion of his readers. I must note, I am not attempting to compare the quality of Danté's poetry with that of Lucado's prose. I am only intending to highlight that the interlacing of fiction and nonfiction narratives, and the expectation that this practice will be effective, particularly as a means of strengthening devotion, has a long history in the Christian tradition. See chapters 3 and 4 in Peter Hawkins, *Danté's Testaments: Essays in Scripture Imagination* (Stanford University Press), 1999.

13 Wells, *Improvisation*, 45, 46.

lens necessary to account for that formation because dramatic discourse offers us a way to account for the movement from text to narrative to the embodied actions that enact those narratives.

MacIntyre argues that narrative on its own represents a community's collective historical memory.[14] By that he means that it represents the story the community tells about itself and the meaning they have collectively made out of the collections of their shared experiences. As such narrative can be said to represent the aesthetic condensation of the meaning they have made of their experiences. As the individual moral agent embodies the practices of the community, they also enact the narrative of that community's history. They dramatically render the meanings of their stories and meaning-making projects through their actions. Therefore human action must necessarily be understood as a set of enacted narratives.[15] Correspondingly, with performance, narrative moves from stories and texts to actions physically embodied in the world. The extent to which these actions faithfully represent the community's notions of virtuous performances, and ultimately its understanding of the good life, reveals the extent to which the community's virtues have become instilled in the moral agent. However, this focus on performance does not displace the significance of narrative within the virtue ethic framework. It simply extends the importance of narrative to the bodies of those enacting the narratives.

Within the context of Christian communities the question of the nature of these performances is generally understood in a continuum between theological and ecclesiological lenses; that is they are generally understood as rooted in the story or narrative of its doctrines (primarily theological) or in the practices of the church (primarily ecclesiological). There are many Christian theologians and ethicists

14 MacIntyre, *After Virtue*, 121.

15 MacIntyre, *After Virtue*, 145, 211. MacIntyre further notes that, with the exception of fictional narratives, stories are lived before they are told (212). The upshot is that for MacIntyre performance necessarily precedes narrative. This speaks to the argument that I am ultimately making that each serves to form the other.

who privilege one approach over the other. However, Christian performance must be rooted both in the traditions necessary for the formation of practices and in the principal narrative responsible for the formation of the Christian imagination, namely the Scriptures.

Theologian Stanley Hauerwas privileges the ecclesiological approach and the role played by the community of the church, expressed through its liturgies, in the moral agent's performance. Noting the important role played by the community of the church in the formation of virtue, Stanley Hauerwas argues that the Christian community is best framed as the community capable of hearing God's story and faithfully re-embodying that story in the world.[16] Put another way, members of that community are those whose imaginations have been so saturated with the gospel narrative that it reveals itself in their actions, relative to the extent of that saturation. Consequently, he argues that the church's ethical task "is to be the kind of community that tells and tells rightly the story of Jesus."[17] For Hauerwas this is accomplished dramatically as the church's practices and actions render this story visible; that is, as it enacts its own performance of the dramatic elements that are representative of the kingdom of justice and peace revealed through the narrative of Jesus's life, death, and resurrection.[18] Indeed he later argues that as the church essentially improvises these performances, it repeats Jesus's own performance, emulating and extending it.[19] Employing a musical metaphor, the church's contextual re-enactment of the gospel narrative becomes a variation of that narrative. Hauerwas demonstrates the important role narrative plays in shaping the church's performance and practices, particularly as it is embedded

16 Hauerwas, *Community of Character*, 1.

17 Hauerwas, *Community of Character* , 52.

18 Hauerwas, *The Peaceable Kingdom*, 99,100.

19 Stanley Hauerwas, *Performing the Faith: Bonhoeffer and the Practice of Nonviolence* (Wipf and Stock, 2004), 103. Hauerwas also argues that the church's ability to persuade those outside of the church with this dramatic rendering of the gospel will depend upon the extent to which they render a faithful performance of the gospel (78).

the church's liturgies. In doing so he hints at the aesthetic processes embedded in these liturgies and practices that work to form Christian affections, imaginations, and dispositions. Hauerwas is not alone in this privileging of this ecclesiological approach to the formation of Christian performance.

James K. A. Smith also queries the church's liturgical practices for evidence of both the affective power of narrative and the affective power inherent in performing that narrative. He frames the practices associated with liturgies, which within a Christian framework would include Eucharist, singing, prayer, teaching, and preaching. The postures used in these practices, as compressed narratives, are the performances that recruit the imagination through the body.[20] Drawing on the scholarship of Maurice Merleau-Ponty and Pierre Bourdieu, he writes, "And insofar as we are immersed bodily into these microperformances, we are, over time, incorporated into a Story that then becomes the script that we implicitly act out. The Story becomes the background narrative and aesthetic orientation that habitually shapes how we constitute our world. We don't memorize the Story as told to us; we imbibe the Story as we perform it in a million little gestures."[21] He goes on to conclude that there can be no pedagogical formation without the repeated performance of these narratives.[22] This includes moral formation. Smith here essentially extends Hauerwas's insights into the role narrative and the aesthetic play in in the individual's moral formation, explicitly rendering what Hauerwas had left implicit.

William Dyrness provides an example of the affective power of enacted narrative within ecclesial practices in his book *Reformed Theology and Visual Culture*. In his book, Dyrness is not endeavoring to account for pedagogical or moral formation. Instead, he is working to describe the Calvinist or Reformed aesthetic, which he frames as a partial interiorization of the visual aspects of Roman Catholic

20 Smith, *Imagining the Kingdom*, 137.
21 Smith, *Imagining the Kingdom*, 110.
22 Smith, *Imagining the Kingdom*, 183.

worship, particularly as those liturgical images related to God's glory. He argues that Calvin's aesthetic encouraged the Christian to visualize that which could not be seen physically, particularly as it relates to the divine, exclusively within the mind's eye, or imagination.[23] Thus Calvin's effort to exchange the medieval liturgical visual culture with the preaching of the word reflects a theologically rooted set of aesthetic commitments.[24] These aesthetic commitments become narrative as the practices of Calvin's church, embedded in its liturgies, become bodily instantiations of these commitments. Eucharist, baptism, prayer, and homilies become embodied performances of Calvin's austere theological aesthetics. Interestingly, and perhaps in spite of Calvin's own intention to privilege the rational over the affective, this theological framework becomes aesthetically instilled in those who repeatedly participate in and perform these Calvinist liturgies. One might even say that the worshipper becomes a Calvinist as much aesthetically, through these performances, as they do theologically through the proclamation of the word. This is significant because the development of this Calvinist aesthetic provides a glimpse into the formational power of narrative and the aesthetic to form even those who desire to marginalize that type of embodied formation (those who would privilege the rational and apparently disembodied to the affective and embodied). On the other hand, there are those who would counter that the narrative and practices of the church are not rooted in the worshipping community and tradition alone. They argue that the Christian's formational narratives and practices must find their root in the narratives recorded in the scriptures. Within this framework, Christian formation can only thrive as those scriptural narratives are faithfully enacted.

Here Kevin Vanhoozer is helpful in articulating the important role played instead by theology and doctrine as they direct the church's

---

23 See chapter 3: "Calvin: Seeing God in the Preached Word" in William Dyrness, *Reformed Theology and Visual Culture* (Cambridge University Press), 2004.

24 Dyrness, *Reformed Theology and Visual Culture*, 68.

performance. He frames the church as the theatre of the gospel and argues, "Theology is the art and science of enacting the mind of Christ everywhere, at all times, and to everyone."[25] For Vanhoozer, "Doctrine, then, is not simply an inert body of knowledge; rather, it intends an active bodily doing."[26] Vanhoozer's approach is not directly concerned with questions of ethics, but is dealing with questions of hermeneutics and scriptural authority and their dramatic articulation. However, in a manner similar to Hauerwas and Smith, Vanhoozer pictures the church as essentially a parable of the kingdom of God. In contrast to both Hauerwas and Smith, Vanhoozer roots the performance that dramatically reveals that kingdom not in the community of faith itself, but in the divine narrative recorded in the Christian Scriptures.[27] He argues that doctrine is fundamentally theatrical because the Bible is itself theo-dramatic: that is, it is a record of God's actions in and for the world.[28] If the Bible frames God as a performer in the theater of the world, then it follows that the church must understand itself as a performer within the same drama. Vanhoozer does not go as far as to equate Scripture with the notion of the church's script, but he does argue that Scripture provides the basis for all Christian doctrine, and thus what brackets fitting Christian stage directions.

He goes on to imagine the church's gathering for worship, prayer, and teaching as its rehearsal, arguing that this is the church *ad intra* (the church's internal work within the community of faith).

---

25 Vanhoozer, *Faith Speaking Understanding: Performing the Drama of Doctrine* (Westminster John Knox Press, 2014), 5.

26 Vanhoozer, *Faith Speaking Understanding*, 5.

27 Vanhoozer, *Faith Speaking Understanding*, 7.

28 Vanhoozer, *Faith Speaking Understanding*, 20. Vanhoozer goes on to frame this within a trinitarian theology, arguing that the doctrine of the Trinity itself is "a precis of the whole drama" (*Faith Speaking Understanding*, 82). Vanhoozer writes, "To state it axiomatically: the economic Trinity *dramatically represents* the immanent Trinity" (82). Thus for Vanhoozer, the church's performance is not just a re-presentation of the gospel narrative as Hauerwas frames it, but is also a re-presentation of the narrative of intertrinitarian love, which he frames as the core of all divine action.

He writes, "Disciples gather to rehearse: to retell and remember the main action of the play, to study their roles, to learn their lines until they know them by heart, to prepare for witness/performance in the world."[29] As the church leaves these gatherings to perform these doctrinal narratives in the world outside the church, it becomes the church *ad extra* (the church's external work outside of the community of faith), the embodied corporate corollary to the economic Trinity. Here members perform the doctrinal narratives, as they have rehearsed them liturgically, in service to and for the benefit of a world, which is the subject of divine love. So while Vanhoozer articulates the role played by the church and its liturgy in funding the Christian's performance, he still frames that performance as fundamentally theological.

Hauerwas and Vanhoozer along with Smith emphasize the importance of the church and doctrine/theology in their performative constructs. The highlighted differences underscore emphases in the meaning attributed to that performance. In each case, performance represents the enactment of particular narratives. Therefore, regardless of the manner in which it is framed ecclesiologically or theologically, performance is as integral as narrative in naming the processes that generate moral formation and virtue within a virtue ethic framework. Performance represents the enactment of the narratives that have formed the moral agent; it is an enactment of that formation as it exists in that moment. As Wells notes, the performance of the moral or good life (*eudaimonia*) is about taking the right things for granted.[30] Speaking casuistically, life becomes a series of moral crises resolved by the habits acquired through, in this case, both doctrinal and community practices; or perhaps framed more holistically, by the habits acquired through practices rooted in doctrine and enacted in community.[31]

---

29 Vanhoozer, *Faith Speaking Understanding*, 140.

30 Wells, *Improvisation*, 76.

31 Wells, *Improvisation*, 77.

The categories of narrative and performance are foundational to the understanding of the processes that facilitate moral formation within virtue ethic discourse. They are foundational to the self-understanding of the formation of virtue within the moral agent as well as to understanding the dynamics that drive that formation. The categories of narrative and performance are also key to understanding the aesthetic and dramatic processes at the core of moral formation.

VIRTUE ETHICS AND THE ELEMENTS OF THE AESTHETIC

The aesthetic is the space where sensual perception and culture intertwine. Using David Morgan's description of this space, the aesthetic represents the "sensuous, imagined, embodied experience of meaning whose significance is measured in feeling no less than intellectual content."[32] The aesthetic here is the embodied cultural interpretation (meaning) of sensory perception, and because of this must be rendered through material, visual, aural, and olfactory culture. Indeed, the notion of culture itself assumes the material representation of meaning. As William Dyrness notes, "Culture is always what we humans make of creation."[33] The aesthetic is then read by the individual through the eyes of the communities in which they have been enculturated.[34] These pieces of material culture represent physical objects that require embodied perception and evoke an embodied response from

32 Morgan, "Protestant Visual Piety and the Aesthetics of American Mass Culture," in *Mediating Religion*, ed. Jolyon Mitchell and Sophia Marriage (T&T Clark, 2003), 107.

33 William Dyrness, *Poetic Theology: God and the Poetics of Everyday Life* (Eerdmans, 2011), 21.

34 Morgan goes on to argue in the same essay that cited earlier in the paragraph the artifacts that make up these material cultures evoke particular responses in those who interact with them. Focusing on these artifacts as they manifest themselves in religious or liturgical settings, he argues that they evoke "1) an emotion that is religiously compelling 2) the experience of a personal address and the need for response 3) a sense of presence or relatedness to another

the subject. Because the encounter with the aesthetic is fundamentally embodied, it also represents the creation of a space in which the affective processing of that encounter is encouraged and anticipated. Thus, an outcome unique to the sphere of the aesthetic is its capacity to initiate an often culturally specific affective response in the subject in relation to a piece of material culture. This aesthetic framework shapes the role of narrative and performance, and thus the body, in the processes of moral formation as envisioned in virtue ethic discourse.

The virtue ethic framework is aesthetic in two particular ways. First, virtue ethics relies on the body and the senses for the processes responsible for moral formation. The processes necessary for habituation are innately embodied, requiring all of the senses and bodily repetition from the moral agent as a means of forming the agent's moral disposition. Second, virtue ethics frames itself as an innately social, and thus an innately cultural process. The virtue ethic framework requires a community of moral agents whose moral agency is in some way inchoate and thus in the process of being formed by and for one another. Thus the processes that constitute moral formation within a virtue ethic framework require individual and community interpretation of sensual perception. These are also the same processes that fund the aesthetic framework. Therefore the attempt to answer the question of how the aesthetic helps us to understand moral formation within a virtue ethic framework must be accomplished first through the lens of sensual perception, and then through the lens of its aesthetic partner: culture.

Sensual Perception

Several scholars who advocate for virtue ethics as the privileged approach to ethical discourse hint at its aesthetic nature.[35] Though

person, a community or God 4) a special mindfulness of or attention to a sacred moment, place or object" ("Protestant Visual Piety," 107, 108).

35 Hauerwas, for instance, notes of Christian ethics in *The Peaceable Kingdom*, "Its first task is to help us rightly envision the world" (29). Hauerwas himself notes novelist Iris Murdoch's simultaneously aesthetic and dramatic

they do not argue for the development of virtue by aesthetic means they do imagine that virtue is achieved through the senses of the moral agent. This growth in virtue subsequently helps form the senses to rightly perceive the actions of other moral agents in the world around them. The aesthetic and meaning making then play important roles in moral formation. It was previously established that narratives, be they fiction or nonfiction, train our perceptive apparatus to perceive the world in a manner that is consistent with that formational narrative. In other words, the narratives we privilege represent the most significant determinative factors in forming the meaning we make of the material and social stimuli we encounter, and in shaping our perception of the proper practical and moral bodily response to those stimuli.

This moral formation then represents a somewhat circular relationship between aesthetic texts/narratives and the senses that perceive them. People create narratives that are aesthetic texts available to the senses, which audiences perceive and engage. The meaning they make of those narratives is dependent upon the formation of their perceptive apparatus to that point. Their perception in the future of something like right and wrong will be directly rooted in the meaning that individual makes of their current perceptions. In this way the shape and content of the narratives one engages are understood through the lenses of the narratives one already loves and the new narratives one engages help to configure the shape of those loves moving forward. In this way, the senses rule supreme, structuring and organizing all questions of meaning.[36] The senses

---

influence in regards to the necessity of vision in the process of moral formation: "her emphasis on vision as the hallmark of the moral life struck me as exactly what I was missing from most accounts of the virtues." (xxiii). He goes on to argue that "the enterprise of Christian ethics primarily helps us to see" (29). While these are both minor points within his larger argument, they represent a rudimentary recognition of the point for which I am arguing, a point Hauerwas leaves undeveloped.

36 Flannery O'Connor highlights the role of the aesthetic within narrative when she writes in *Mystery and Manners*, "Fiction begins where human knowledge begins—with the senses—and every fiction writer is bound by this

are integral to the formation of our perceptions and ultimately the shape of our moral activity.

Seeing then is an embodied practice related to narrative.[37] Meaning making is then also a fundamentally embodied practice rooted

---

fundamental aspect of his medium" (42). In another essay she reinforces this notion: "The fact is that the materials of the fiction writer are the humblest. Fiction is about everything human and we are made of dust, and if you scorn getting yourself dusty, then you shouldn't be a fiction writer" (68). To this end, O'Connor writes in *Mystery and Manners*, "I know a good many fiction writers who paint, not because they're any good at painting, but because it helps their writing. It forces them to look at things. Fiction writing is very seldom a matter of saying things; it is a matter of showing things" (93). O'Connor notes that the writer's job is to employ their perceptive apparatus to fulfill Joseph Conrad's dictum that the novelist should render the greatest possible justice to the visible universe (80). Conrad himself writes, "My task which I am trying to achieve is, by the power of the written word, to make you hear, to make you feel—it is, before all to make you see. That—and no more, and it is everything. If I succeed, you shall find there, according to your deserts, encouragement, consolation, fear, charm, all you demand—and perhaps, also the glimpse of truth for which you have forgotten to ask." Joseph Conrad, *The N***** of the Narcissus*, 1898, https://www.gutenberg.org/cache/epub/17731/pg17731-images.html.

37 David Morgan is helpful here in articulating the relationship between vision, the senses, the larger social body, and moral formation in his book *The Embodied Eye*. Morgan argues that seeing is an innately embodied process that is neither isolated from a person's other senses, nor from the larger social body (xvii). For Morgan, this bonded pair of body and the image also links the body to the affective power of narrative, here instantiated in the image and enacted visually. As an example of this interstice he draws on Albrecht Dürer's woodcuts of scenes from the biblical narrative. Morgan observes, "The mystery of images lies in the subtle slippage from *was* to *is*. But it takes a disposition for this to happen" (36). This slippage relies on the apparent or perhaps imagined passage of time necessary in narrative. Here as the viewer with a particularly devotional disposition considers the image, they appropriate it and construct a meaning in relation to their personal devotional commitments and dispositions, and the devotional commitments and dispositions of the communities in which they participate and belong, which are rooted in the narratives they privilege. One nests their reading of the narrative embedded in the image in relation to (alongside or perhaps even in opposition to) the community's narrative appropriation of that same image (depending on their relationship to that community, and their affection for the competing counternarratives privileged by the other communities in which they participate). In either case,

in narrative and the senses. The narrative processes that are fundamental to the formation of the moral agent within the virtue ethics framework are also fundamentally dependent upon sight and by extension all the other senses fundamental to embodiment. Both narrative and sensual perception rely on the senses and aid to develop the moral agent's perceptive apparatus and the meaning he makes of that sensual perception. Additionally, both narrative and sensual perception rely not only on the agent as he participates in the formation of his own moral dispositions, but also on the community and their narratives which are also forming them. If this is the case, then we must also account for the social forces at work in these sensual processes, more specifically the role played by culture and thus community in the aesthetics of moral formation.

Culture

The aesthetic, as it relates to the institutions associated with the fine arts, philosophies, and theologies of beauty, and the practices that grow out of these endeavors and arguments, are embedded in cultural processes that are constructed to help individuals and communities construct meaning out of their sensed perception of the world. In short the aesthetic is as social as it is sensual, which means that seeing is an innately social activity. David Morgan notes, "To see, in other words, is to see for oneself, but also with others, and thereby to see with the eyes of a social body."[38] Seeing here is a practice that is simultaneously biological and social.

If, as Hauerwas argues, the formation of virtue in the individual is best framed as a gift from the community in which they are embedded, and that process, as I am arguing, is best understood within an aesthetic-dramatic framework, then there are aesthetic processes at play in that formation. Employing this aesthetic lens retroactively, the

---

this process of narrative meaning making began with and is rooted in the senses, and thus the body.

38 Morgan, *The Embodied Eye*, 55.

dramatic takes on a new light; that is to say it reads differently when read through both an aesthetic and dramatic lens simultaneously. For example, the dramatic rendering of narrative emblematic of the church's performance can be read as its own aesthetic text. This is because narrative fundamentally engages the senses and thus the imagination. Thus an embodied performance of a particular narrative or set of narratives can also be framed aesthetically and read as its own aesthetic text: that is as a narrative performance available to the senses and thus subject to the individual's reading of that performance as its own aesthetic text. These narrative enactments could be any embodied enactment of the individual or community's vision of the good life, such as liturgical narratives (such as the Eucharist), moral narratives, or even the enactment of the values instantiated in fictional narratives. In each case, the one perceiving the performance is seeing and reading it—perceiving it as one embedded in a particular interpretive community. They are making meaning of that performance as they would make meaning out of any other aesthetic text or fictional narrative. In this way, the performance of a particular narrative both affectively instills that narrative into the performer and renders it aesthetically visible to those both inside and outside of the community, opening the potential of affectively imparting that same narrative in the one viewing the performance.[39]

Thus this process of forming the individual's performance (and subsequently their virtue as it is understood by their community) can itself be framed as a narrative performance of a particular vision of the good life that has been embedded in her affections and dispositions through simultaneously aesthetic and dramatic processes. If this is an accurate description of the processes that form the moral agent, then we can employ this framework as a means of gauging the relationship between Evangelical material culture and the practices

39 In this vein Hauerwas notes, "The intelligibility (and hence the persuasiveness) of Christian faith springs not from independently formulated criteria, but from compelling renditions, faithful performances" (*Performing the Faith*, 78).

that are fundamental to its social and material locations and the formations they cultivate.

EVANGELICAL AESTHETIC TEXTS AND MORAL FORMATION

To consider the manner in which Evangelical aesthetic texts and practices shape the virtues of those engaging these texts and participating in these practices, root these practices within an aesthetic framework. Consider the manner in which the practice engages the participant's senses and the social and cultural lenses employed by the participants to make sense of these practices. To that end, the presence and formational action of the components constitute the aesthetic framework. Consider whether and how these texts and practices (and practices as texts) may be forming the imaginations, dispositions, and subsequent practices of their Evangelical participants.

CHAPTER 4

Performance and the Dramatics of Moral Formation

> We cannot learn the story by doing exactly what others did, for we cannot do exactly what they did. Rather, we must let their lives imaginatively challenge our own, so that we may learn how to embody the virtues which determined not only what they did, but how they did it.
>
> —Stanley Hauerwas, *The Peaceable Kingdom: A Primer in Christian Ethics*

The processes that fund moral formation are rooted in the aesthetic. Formation is most deeply rooted in one's loves, affections, and desires. One's actions and practices grow from and influence one's affections and dispositions, which then in a circular fashion become a part of reinforcing one's actions and practices. Those actions and practices represent a dramatic rendering, or a performance, of those affections and dispositions. More specifically the moral agent's practices enact the affections and dispositions cultivated through their engagement with aesthetic texts and material culture. These aesthetic and ethical frameworks can be widened to include the dramatic because they share common roots in the body and because aesthetic perception and dramatic action form and reinforce one another. A person's practices represent performances of the visions of the good life instantiated in beloved aesthetic texts and pieces of material culture. Stated simply, practices render aesthetic commitments visible through dramatic action.

PRACTICES AS DRAMATIC RENDERINGS OF THE AESTHETIC

Dramatic action offers a way of understanding practices aesthetically. The inclusion of dramatic discourse accounts for the role the aesthetic plays in moral formation, at least in part, because dramatic discourse is partially rooted in aesthetic discourse. The aesthetic is the interlacing of sensual perception and culture. The dramatic is built on the same interlacing, but also adds threads of performance and narrative. The dramatic thus represents an expansion of the aesthetic. To understand this relationship, imagine these elements interacting along two axes: (1) the performance and the embodiment necessary for that performance, and (2) the narrative processes that fund human projects of making meaning. The affections formed in moral agents along these axes represent their aesthetic commitment that shapes their social, devotional, and political commitments. These aesthetic commitments create a lens that filters and arranges perceptions before any rational decisions come into play. These are the assessments that rational choices and articulations often rationalize. The dramatic, then, is the embodied expression, or performance, of one's love and affections that have been instilled through the development of one's aesthetic commitments.[1]

1 I argued earlier that dramatic performances also represent their own set of aesthetic texts, rendering aesthetic commitments visible through narrative action. The argument that the dramatic represents the narrative performance of aesthetic commitments does not negate that argument but complements it. Here I am endeavoring to describe the performative portion of this formational circle, and the manner in which practices are formed through aesthetic texts, be they created or enacted.

Embodiment and Performance

As a medium that has aesthetic roots, the dramatic is dependent upon and embedded in the materiality of creation.[2] Theologically speaking, humans are physical creations designed to exist and thrive in a material/physical world. Both the dramatic and the aesthetic exist as denizens of the physical world, open and available to human senses. The aesthetic is wedded to the sensing of physical reality. This is true both of the materiality of objects created through means of human agency (art, crafts, and other pieces of material culture) and the materiality of the natural world (objects unaffected by the intentionality of human agency). On this point philosopher Hans Georg Gadamer notes in his essay "The Relevance of the Beautiful" that "it is not only in the face of art that we enjoy this aesthetic experience, but in the presence of nature as well."[3] This means that a person's experience of the aesthetic is rooted in its materiality, not in the nature of its crafting.

Similarly, the dramatic is necessarily perceptible to the senses, but movement and performance is added to the perception of material objects. Thus, the dramatic does not just point to the physicality fundamental to the aesthetic but embodies that physicality. In doing so the dramatic represents the fundamental embeddedness of the body in the materiality of creation. Just as an aesthetic object physically instantiates and memorializes the aesthetic commitments of the one or ones who created it, so actions physically embody the individual's affections, dispositions, and habits. In both cases this is only possible because expressions of both the aesthetic and the dramatic are embedded in the materiality of the physical world. The body, as it is embedded in the materiality of the world, is necessary for the

---

2 As theologian Trevor Hart notes, "To be human is to be wedded inexorably to and part of a material creation, even if our humanity will not submit to any accounting conducted in material terms alone" (Trevor Hart, "Beyond Theatre and Incarnation," in *Theatrical Theology: Explorations in Performing the Faith*, ed. Wesley Vander Lugt and Trevor Hart [Cascade Books, 2014], 31).

3 Hans-Georg Gadamer, *The Relevance of the Beautiful and Other Essays*, ed. Robert Bernasconi (Cambridge University Press, 1986), 30.

perception of the physical world. Understood within this framework, the body is necessary to perceive both particular aesthetic texts and dramatic action.

In addition, the body's material embeddedness fundamentally requires dramatic action from humans. Existing as a physical being in a material reality requires all types of dramatic acts. Thus, when a person uses their senses to perceive either an aesthetic object such as a painting or a dramatic action such as the giving of a speech, they are employing the body and the senses to perform. For example, according to theologian Jim Fodor, something as basic as reading can be framed as a dramatic act. Fodor applies this observation to the reading of Scripture: "Thankfully, the world of acting and theatrical plays reminds all of us, but theologians especially, of the overtly physical dimensions of reading. Drama demonstrates palpably how reading is unavoidably a bodily process."[4] In Fodor's example he recognizes that humans employ their senses, and therefore their body, to perform an act of reading. Ultimately, this of course is not just a reference to the reading of written texts, but also to the reading of aesthetic texts and the dramatic action that take place in the theater of the world. The body is continually reading objects, texts, and other bodies in motion.

This embodiment necessarily then extends beyond the act of reading to the act of writing and creating as well. The aesthetic is

---

4 Jim Fodor, "The Play of Christian Life: When Wisdom Calls to Wisdom," in Lugt and Hart, *Theatrical Theology*, 148. This is important, because as David Morgan notes in *The Embodied Eye*, images themselves enact their own presence. He writes, "Any image may act as a trace of its original, sharing with it some aspect of its being, even if only enough to *promise* the power of overcoming absence" (29). Alongside bodies, aesthetic texts are performing for the viewer—in this instance performing presence. However, the aesthetic text can perform myriad other functions and identities. In each case they perform sets of aesthetic commitments that are made available to all the senses. Here David Morgan notes, "The *embodied eye* means that seeing is never independent of touching, feeling, and the manipulation of the body and the environment; and the study of religious seeing is the study of embodiment" (54). In this way, one could argue that each aesthetic text embodies its own dramatic action.

fundamentally dramatic (and the dramatic fundamentally aesthetic) in that aesthetic texts depend on physical performances for their creation.[5] For example, a painting, film, or musical recording is the unchanging monument to the gestures necessary to create them. They represent the product of the performance of a set of dramatic actions.[6] At its most basic level this is dramatic action revealing the aesthetic and making it available to the senses. Thus, a reinforcing circle exists: The aesthetic is the product and embodiment of the dramatic action necessary for its creation, and the dramatic is the active embodiment of particular sets of aesthetic commitments that are rooted in one's affections and dispositions. In either sense the effect that aesthetic objects or dramatic actions have on the one engaging them is achieved as the viewer perceives it through their senses and their body.

Meaning Making and Narrative

In addition to their physical roots, both the aesthetic and dramatic share ontological roots. Both represent material instantiations of the human impulse to make meaning out of their experiences of the materiality in which they are embedded.[7] Recall Mark

5 Philosopher Jean François Lyotard in his essay "Gesture and Commentary" provides helpful observations on this point. Writing of artists who expect their work to take part in the discourse specific to the institution of the fine arts and theater, he argues that as a part of the processes that set their work aside to this end, the artist expects the critic and philosopher to "transcribe their gestus." That is the artist expects the critic and philosopher to interpret the manner in which their body has interacted with a given medium to create a visual or audible record of the gestures necessary to produce the work (Jean François Lyotard, "Gesture and Commentary," in *Between Ethics and Aesthetics: Crossing the Boundaries*, ed. Dorata Glowacka and Stephen Boos [State University of New York Press, 2002], 74).

6 In this way, Lyotard notes, "the work of gesture is still an event" (*Between Ethics and Aesthetics*, 80).

7 This observation on the nature of the relationship between the physical world and human meaning making also has theological implications, since, theologically speaking, there exist both seen and unseen portions of reality. As

Johnson's notion, "That what we call 'mind' and what we call 'body' are not two things, but rather aspects of one organic process, so that all our meaning, thought, and language emerge from the aesthetic dimensions of this embodied activity."[8] Therefore, "meaning is not just what is consciously entertained in acts of feeling and thought; instead, meaning reaches deep down into our corporeal encounter with our environment."[9] Practices, as dramatic action, render the meaning embodied in one's aesthetic commitments viscerally visible through performances available to the senses.

One's practices dramatically reveal their aesthetic commitments while simultaneously further shaping them as its own aesthetic text. In fact the only way to truly know a person's aesthetic commitments is through their dramatic action. Because of this, the practices that reveal a Christian individual or community's aesthetic commitments are not limited to only liturgical acts. While they do include practices such as worship and the embodied rituals associated with it, they would also include practices such as acts of service,; the practices associated with the engagement of aesthetic texts and pieces of material culture, such as books, television shows, TikToks, movies, and music; and the purchasing practices broadly associated with consumerism, including the purchase of both Christian and secular products. In each of these sets of practices dramatic action is necessary to both perform and reveal the meaning latent in the individual and community's aesthetic commitments. Thus, the overlap between

---

William Dyrness notes in *Poetic Theology*, "I will argue that symbolic practices of this kind can also be 'theological' in the broad sense of the word. That is, they are places where, because God's continuing presence in creation and God's redemptive work in Christ and by the Spirit, God is also active, nurturing, calling, and drawing persons—and indeed, all creation—toward the perfection God intends for them" (6). Here the making of meaning is embedded in the bodily dramatic actions necessary for enacting rituals which allows the one enacting them to encounter an environment, a reality, where the physical and the spiritual are interlaced.

8 Johnson, *The Meaning of the Body: Aesthetics of Human Understanding* (University of Chicago Press, 2007), 1.

9 Johnson, *Meaning of the Body*, 25.

the aesthetic and dramatic represent spaces where the performer's actions reveal their aesthetic commitments, rendering them visible.[10]

As an example, imagine a parent who desires that their son participate in an organized church ministry that serves families with material needs for the purpose of developing empathy; that parent is projecting a set of meanings into that child's life. At a basic level, they are projecting aesthetic commitments regarding one's right relationship to the materiality of creation and the cultural products humans make of it. These are commitments, for example, that view that materiality in terms of property and exclusive ownership. They are projecting an aesthetic and moral commitment to sharing portions of the property one owns with those who own comparatively less property. They are also projecting a commitment that one should not share all of one's material property with those with comparably less property. In addition, within this example, that parent is framing these set of practices as empathetic, an attempt to imagine and share the feelings and concerns of those with material needs,

10 Theologian William Dyrness recognizes something like this in his book *Senses of the Soul*, which examines the formational role played by the senses and the aesthetic in Christian worship. He argues that a church's visual culture and worship practices shape the devotional, theological, and social dispositions of the worshipper (William Dyrness, *Senses of the Soul: Art and the Visual in Christian Worship* [Cascade Books, 2008], 5). Because this experience of ecclesial visual cultural is embedded within worship practices, Dyrness observes, "this implies that strategies of visual interpretation have to be hermeneutically expanded to include, for example, the impact of dramatic activity, what in religious terms is called 'ritual'" (6). He goes on to affirm both the aesthetic and dramatic processes that are fundamental to formation even in Protestant contexts where the function of the visual and the aesthetic is intentionally minimized (162, 163). See also chapter 3: "Calvin: Seeing God in the Preached Word," in *Reformed Theology and Visual Culture*. Here Dyrness proposes that Protestants tend to foster an intense inward focus that privileges aural stimuli and encourages the worshipper to recreate the visual aspects of particular scriptural narratives as a part of their individual and corporate devotional practices. In short, even in contexts intent on minimizing the formational role played by the aesthetic, sensual perception remains a key part of the worshipper's devotional formation because of their fundamental embeddedness in the materiality of the world.

while attempting to offer a form of perceived help within this framework of aesthetic assumptions. Because these commitments and others embody one's commitments to the normative shape of one's engagement with the materiality of creation, they are fundamentally aesthetic, even if they are simultaneously fundamentally ethical. In this way, that parent is writing a script that both directs their child's actions, and the meaning they would like that child to make of those actions. That script is at least partially rooted in the narratives transmitted through the aesthetic texts that have formed that parents affections and dispositions, and as that child embodies these sets of aesthetic commitments, they will prove formative in their life as well. Furthermore, the meaning that parent is encouraging their child to perform is rooted in the meaning-making project embedded in the aesthetic texts that formed their own affections.

The narrative of meaning making is fundamental to understanding the aesthetic processes that fund moral formation. James K. A. Smith notes, while describing the physically and subsequently narratively embedded nature of meaning making, that "our action is always *en*action—part of a dance of embodiment and our environment, a mode of interaction that is governed and propelled as much (or more!) by our emotional appraisal of our situation as by our rational reflection on it."[11] Human projects of meaning making are

11 Smith, *Imagining the Kingdom*, 38. Smith is writing here of the narratives that shape our perceptive apparatus and our tendency to instinctively re-enact these narratives when they are elicited by particular situations. To that end Smith writes, "Our emotional perceptive apparatus (which I'm linking to 'the imagination') is significantly 'trained' by narrative. I will have implicitly and affectively absorbed stories and narratives and pictures . . . and such 'storied' pedagogy, we'll see, is intimately linked to our embodiment" (36). MacIntyre notes something similar in *After Virtue* arguing that all human actions represent enacted narratives. To that end he writes, "It is because we all live out narratives in our lives and because we understand our lives in terms of the narratives that we live out that the form of narrative is appropriate for understanding the actions of others" (212). This of course would then be axiomatically true as one endeavors to make meaning out of one's own experiences as well. Smith goes on to argue in his book *You Are What You Love* that human action should be fundamentally framed as enaction because "to be human is to be

built upon a foundation of narrative construction; that is, practices represent the performance of narratives embedded in the affections and dispositions of the performer.

The affections and dispositions are formed, in part, through the performer's engagement with the aesthetic texts and material culture that constitute a significant portion of the performer's material and social environment. In this way performances of these narratives become a part of the meaning-making process. If these narratives represent aesthetically embedded teleological visions of the good life, as that good life is understood and articulated by the creator of that text, then the performance of these narratives represents an opportunity for the performer to experience something of that good life through her performance of it.[12] These actions then represent performances of particular visions of the good life that are embedded in the aesthetic texts. As one engages the text or piece of material culture they are invited toward that vision of the good life. They are invited to participate in that vision by imaginatively playing with it, trying it on through their actions.[13] In doing so, they are invited to act out a particular set of meanings. Depending on their prior

---

oriented by some vision of the good life, some picture of what we think counts as 'flourishing.' And we want that. We crave it. We desire it. This is why our most fundamental mode of orientation to the world is love. We are oriented by our longings, directed by our desires. We adopt ways of life that are indexed to such visions of the good life, not usually because we 'think through' our options but rather because some picture captures our imagination" (11).

12 See Smith, *Imagining the Kingdom*, 109.

13 Though not the focus here, it would be fascinating to develop this notion of the relationship between practices and dramatic formation alongside Hans-Georg Gadamer's understanding of the play necessary for an engagement with the aesthetic described in *The Relevance of the Beautiful*. Gadamer writes specifically of engaging an aesthetic text created for the purposes of aesthetic contemplation within the Kantian framework represented by the institution of the fine arts; however, I argue, particularly in light of the manner in which Gadamer includes the natural world in his framing of the human aesthetic experience, that his description can be applied more broadly to include aesthetic texts not created for the institution of the fine arts. Gadamer argues that one must play along with the aesthetic text and its creator in order to facilitate a genuine reception of the text (25, 26). Given what I am arguing is the narrative

formation in relation to other practices and aesthetic texts, they may develop an affection for the new practices and meanings, or they may be disturbed, offended, sickened, or feel uneasy about them. The next steps in their formation depend on the extent to which they develop an affection for and continue to participate in the practices that are forming them.

The repeated performance of practices can be framed as a sort of submission to the meaning and the vision of the good life that is fundamental to the ongoing formation of the participant's affections and dispositions. Furthermore, the aesthetic commitments instantiated in a particular aesthetic text will not become fully embedded in the moral agent's affections and dispositions without participation and the performance of these types of practices. It is the dramatic performance of the practices themselves that are essential for human formation.[14]

---

nature of the aesthetic this could be extended to include the practices generated by the engagement with the aesthetic.

14 This also represents the crux of Smith's argument in his *Cultural Liturgies* trilogy. This aesthetic (and dramatic) process of formation also hews closely to the process of virtue formation envisioned by both Alisdair MacIntyre and Stanley Hauerwas. For them (as well as for Aristotle, as both MacIntyre and Hauerwas embrace Aristotle's formational framework) virtue is dependent upon the practices tjat fund its formation. Furthermore, the practices which perform that virtue come to represent acts finding root in the moral agent's affections and dispositions. MacIntyre in *After Virtue* describes virtue as "an acquired human quality the possession and exercise of which tends to enable us to achieve those goods which are internal to practices and the lack of which effectively prevents us from achieving any such goods" (191). These practices represent the performances necessary to embody the good life. To that end MacIntyre describes the good life as "the life spent in seeking for the good life for [humanity], and the virtues necessary for the seeking are those which will enable us to understand more and what else the good life for [humanity] is" (219). (The brackets represent my replacement of the gender specific "man" with the more inclusive humanity, which represents the intended subject of his description.) He goes on to acknowledge that this notion of the good life, similar to the notion of virtue, is not universal: "I am someone's son or daughter, someone else's cousin or uncle, I am a citizen of this country or that city, a member of this or that guild or profession, I belong to this clan, that tribe, this nations. Hence what is good for me has to be the good for one who inhabits those roles. . . . These constitute for me the given of my life, my moral starting point" (220).

As one performs these visions of the good life embedded in aesthetic texts through repeated practices, one develops affections, dispositions, and virtues that grow to become consistent with the vision of the good life he is enacting. That person comes to dramatically perform the visions of the good life embedded in the aesthetic texts that fund that vision. The moral agent's performance therefore grows out of the human impulse toward meaning making. However, it also funds that meaning making impulse. Furthermore, it also broadens and deepens the sense of the meaning associated with the aesthetic text and the subsequent performance. This is emblematic of dramatic action as a discourse that is constructed on and dependent upon aesthetic discourse. In addition, dramatic action not only performs the notion of the good life embedded in particular sets of aesthetic texts and pieces of material culture but performance is fundamental to the formation of the affections and dispositions of those performing them.

THE PROBLEM OF MALFORMATION

This set of arguments raises the question of the ethical vectors of the aesthetic texts that are forming the moral agent's affections, imagination, disposition, and practices. If one's dramatic performances and practices fundamentally grow out of the affections cultivated by aesthetic means, then the moral trajectory of these texts becomes of utmost importance. If the immoral or evil is aesthetically represented as the good, then those affections, dispositions, and imaginations will grow to axiomatically perceive the immoral or evil as the good. Even if not framed in the stark black and white language of evil and good, the problem of what could be called aesthetic malformation is real. For example, employing a navigational metaphor, within this framework, if one's loves and affections are aesthetically formed twenty degrees askew of what we might call the true north of the good, then the moral agent's ability to perceive the good will be degraded, perhaps even proportionally. Pushing the metaphor a bit, one could start a journey in Dallas intending to arrive in Fargo and end up in Indianapolis. If Fargo represents the true north of the good, Indianapolis here would represent what the individual was formed to believe was the true north of the good. That person would not be able to easily recognize that they have not arrived at the end they believed they set out for.[15] This means that we must account for the fact that all aesthetic formation unavoidably means some degree of malformation. Given the Christian's theological understanding of humanity's brokenness/sinfulness, there is a sense in which these fundamental shortcomings, built into the processes of aesthetic formation, can be understood as the aesthetics of sin. Regardless of how it is framed, this aesthetic malformation must be accounted for.

Included in aesthetic malformations are the creative use of aesthetic texts in ways not intended or envisioned by the creators of the aesthetic texts. With unintended aesthetic formations, there is also a formation that occurs when diverse sets of aesthetic texts pull loves and affections toward competing and even conflicting ends. A single aesthetic text or piece of material culture often instantiates more than one vision of the good life. These differing visions of the good life that emanate from a single text may represent contradictory and competing visions of how things ought to be. For example, the long-running Evangelical television show *The 700 Club*, hosted for decades by evangelist Pat Robertson, before his passing, presently airs on the Freeform cable channel, owned by the Walt Disney Company.[16] The program broadcasts a particular vision of the Christian good life rooted in a markedly conservative (both

---

15 The use of this navigational metaphor of course intends no real life commentary on the goodness, or lack thereof, of any the cities named in the metaphor.

16 This may seem odd at first glance, given that the rest of the content broadcast and streamed by Freeform does not reflect *The 700 Club*'s devotional commitments. This is because the Freeform channel was founded in 1961 as the Christian Broadcasting Network (CBN) in Portsmouth, Virginia. As it moved from terrestrial broadcasting to cable television, it was rebranded as The Family Channel in 1988. CBN sold the channel in 1998 to News Corporation, with the stipulation that it continue to include *The 700 Club* in its daily broadcast schedule on weekdays. After the sale it became Fox Family Channel. Fox Family

theologically and politically) and often theologically Charismatic version of Evangelical theology and culture. The program is a production of the Christian Broadcasting Network (CBN), which describes its work as "a global nonprofit ministry demonstrating the love of God and sharing the Gospel of Jesus Christ through media evangelism and humanitarian aid."[17] However, as a program broadcast on the Freeform network it also instantiates visions of the good life that are rooted in commercial broadcasting (for example, concerns with profitability and ratings). In addition, the program also represents a commodification of the good life that the producers of *The 700 Club* want to share, namely the Christian gospel. Their gospel message is broadcast alongside the other commodities the Freeform channel attempts to sell to consumers. In this way, the average Freeform network viewer could understand *The 700 Club*'s instantiation of the gospel as simply another commodity alongside the cell phones, fast food, and fast fashion being sold on the network. As such it instantiates at least two competing visions of the good life: the one proclaimed by the producers of *The 700 Club* and the vision instantiated in the aesthetics of Freeform's commercial environment. This notion of their competing visions of the good life does not even take into consideration the particular content of the aesthetic texts produced and broadcast by Freeform or *The 700 Club*. Competing visions of the good life instantiated within a single aesthetic text or piece of material culture are not uncommon. These cross currents are endemic to the aesthetic and dramatic.

Another example of these cross currents that are embedded in the material envisioning and the material instantiations of the good life and the practices they cultivate is the mall. James K.A. Smith argues a mall represents both an aesthetic environment, and a material

---

was sold in 2001 to the Walt Disney Company and became the ABC Family Channel. In 2016 Disney rebranded ABC Family as Freeform.

17 "CBN Partners," https://wwwl.cbn.com/cbn-partners, accessed August 1, 2019.

instantiation of culture.[18] Contrast Smith's account of the affections and practices formed by, in, and through the mall with the formational ends envisioned by one of the mall's tenants: Family Christian stores. In their cultural heyday as an occupant of the mall, from the 1980s into the early 2000s, Family Christian stores represented the largest Christian retailer in the United States, peaking at more than 350 retail locations across thirty-nine states. They initially focused on the selling of Christian books under the name Zondervan Book Store and later under the Family Book Store moniker, but expanded to sell Christian music alongside Christian knickknacks, collectibles, and novelties. As a Christian bookseller its goal was the spread of the Christian gospel and the sale of the books that would serve to further Christian discipleship, and the formation of practices in individuals and communities that would accomplish those ends. As citizens of the mall, these stores were also calling Christians into a space that, in Smith's account, was shaping their loves and affections toward visions of the good life associated with consumerism. These conflicting ends represent a glimpse of the cross currents present in the aesthetic processes of formation. They instantiate the simultaneously dramatic and narrative nature of the aesthetic. Because aesthetic texts and pieces of material culture are the product of the gestures necessary to create them, they carry in them a narrative. They memorialize and carry the story of the dramatic action and the aesthetic commitments necessary for their creation.

---

18 He argues in *You Are What You Love* that a mall "offers a rich, embodied visual mode of evangelism that *attracts* us. This is a gospel whose power is *beauty*, which speaks to our deepest desires. It compels us to come, not through dire moralisms, but rather with a winsome invitation to share in this envisioned good life" (43). Describing the process through which the mall attracts its denizens toward a particular vision of the good life he writes, "I don't think my way into consumerism. Rather, I'm covertly conscripted into a way of life because I have been formed by cultural practices. . . . These tangible, visceral, repeated practices carry a story about human flourishing that we learn in unconscious ways. These practices are loaded with their own teleological orientation toward a particular vision of the good life . . . and by our immersion in them we are—albeit unwittingly—being taught what and how to love" (45, 46).

The 700 Club, Freeform, the mall, and Family Christian Stores each carry their aesthetic commitments in their aesthetic texts and in the material culture they create and have formed and continue to form the affections, dispositions, and practices of those who engage them toward each's particular, if conflicting, ends. To be a Christian (or just a human) embedded in the materiality of creation and the sociality of culture is to experience a diverse set of aesthetic texts and pieces of material culture competing for one's affections and endeavoring to form one's practices. To quote the Canadian indie rock band Fast Romantics, "Everybody's Trying to Steal Your Heart."[19] These instances represent just a glimpse of the aesthetic texts vying for our affections, but they also offer insight into the contested space that is aesthetic formation.

Finally, malformation. To employ the notion of malformation, one must start with a normative notion of formation. Virtue ethics does not fundamentally carry in it these normative notions of virtue; it represents an approach that desires to understand the processes by which one becomes a virtuous person, regardless of how one might understand virtue. Even as a Christian who would seek to find ethical norms in Scripture and theology, notions of virtue can represent a contested space. Articulating normativity represents a space where Christians through the centuries have done their best to make sense of the Old and New Testament's ethical claims on the Christians behavior and practices. The question of what constitutes scriptural ethical normativity of course will not be settled here.

However, leaning on the church's accounts of ethical normativity through the ages, there is a broadly sketched imagining of Christian normativity. By all accounts, these articulations of Christian ethical normativity would commonly exclude the domination, oppression, and degradation of their fellow human beings made in the image of God. The church, of course, even as it might not argue that these behaviors were ethical, has commonly engaged in practices

19 Fast Romantics, "Everybody's Trying to Steal Your Heart," track 1 on *American Love*, self-released, 2017.

that embody these ethical failures. It has also at times been morally formed in such a way that the practices associated with the domination, oppression, and degradation of people was fashioned in such a way that they fit within the bounds of normative Christian ethical practices. Theologian Willie James Jennings offers an account of the aesthetic processes that funded this exact type of moral formation. To that end, he identifies and deconstructs the formation of the racial imagination, which he argues was formed by self-identified Christians through aesthetic processes. Jennings notes that from the beginnings of the colonial projects in Portugal in the fifteenth century, "being white placed one at the center of the symbolic and real reordering of space."[20] To Jennings, this runs counter to what he understands to be a biblical imagining of people and places where God is revealed as the Creator of all people and materiality.[21] Jennings argues that colonial Europeans were able to socially and ultimately materially reconfigure indigenous spaces away from these doctrinal and aesthetic commitments to the universally divine origins of people and materiality by essentially renarrating and thus reframing both the material and the social meaning of land and flesh. Jennings emphasizes the power of this narrative reframing of the materiality of creation on the colonial imagination.[22] The colonial renarration of the materiality of creation functions similarly, establishing whiteness as the colonial aesthetic anchor, and forming all imaginations,

---

20 Jennings, *The Christian Imagination*, 59.

21 Jennings, *The Christian Imagination*, 212, 213. Jennings cites Isaac Watts's replacement of Israel with Great Britain in his translation of the Psalms, arguing that this supersessionism is indicative of the colonial project. Just as colonial logic reorients the relationship of people to land, subverting it and making commodities of both the people and the land, so here it essentially unlands Israel. Land is thus to the colonial imagination, "first a matter of possession and second, if at all, of signification" (218).

22 He quotes literary critic Pascale Casanova, who compares this narrative space to the prime meridian, which is itself an arbitrary, fictive line, but "contributes to the real organization of the world" (228).

dispositions, and practices around this aesthetic commitment.[23] Because those responsible for these aesthetic reorientations identify themselves as Christians, Christian theology becomes bound to the confines of this social imagination as well, particularly as it commits to the primary legitimacy of the central European powers narrating these reorientations.[24]

Jennings's description of the processes that formed the racial imaginations, perceptions, affections, and practices of colonials, indigenous, and African peoples represent exactly the same set of aesthetic processes that have been described thus far, except they have formed those affections and practices toward ends inconsistent with any good faith interpretation of the text of the Bible, askew from the true north of the good. In doing so, Jennings offers a description of the dark side of the aesthetic formational process. In considering how Evangelicals are formed by the aesthetic texts they engage and love, keep in mind that not all formation is for the better. The notion of aesthetic formation only describes the process by which affections and practices are formed. Once that description is accomplished, one must also consider the shape and trajectory of that formation.

---

23 See Jennings, *The Christian Imagination*, 229–31. To that end, he notes, "however, as I showed with the southern household, there was a geographic expansion of identity around the body of the master, the body of whiteness. Herein lay the other aspect of the problem that helped to generate segregated mentality within Christian Imagination, that is, a world forced inside the intimacy of white existence" (241).

24 Jennings, *The Christian Imagination*, 232, 233.

CHAPTER 5

Operation Christmas Child and Evangelical Formation

> We developed a love for Operation Christmas Child. Once you start, it's in your heart. We're going to keep doing it.
>
> —Cindy Koontz, "Franklin Graham Stops in Dallas on Tour of Shoebox Processing Centers"

Every year as summer winds down and American children begin returning to school, many Evangelical churches and community's thoughts turn toward young children outside of the United States. Gatherings are organized, committees are convened, and plans are made to fill and send shoeboxes full of toys, toiletries, and school supplies around the globe that are then opened by children on Christmas morning. Families in the US arrange days to purchase these toys and supplies, which then become yearly events, and eventually, traditions. Churches gather to fill these boxes and to pray for, celebrate, and commission the sendoff of the boxes. This is Operation Christmas Child (OCC). For many American Evangelical Christians, over the past twenty-five years, participation in this ministry has become as deeply ingrained in their constellation of fall activities as football or Thanksgiving. OCC is a beloved ministry, and an activity that participants look forward to returning to every year.

The affections that are shared by and that are formed in OCC participants are cultivated over time as participants return annually to these clusters of practices. They are cultivated through church services, social gatherings, and shopping trips. They are also formed and embodied amid the production of posters, books, videos, and other forms of material culture. These aesthetic texts and pieces of material culture, both purchased and created, animate participant's practices through the formation of their affections and imaginations. Understanding these affections is key to understanding the success of OCC. And understanding the manner in which these affections are translated into dispositions and practices is fundamental to understanding Evangelical moral development and identity.

OCC was founded in 1990 by businessman Dave Cooke as a venture to provide Christmas presents to orphans in Romania. By 1995 it had expanded its operation to include Bosnia, Croatia, Serbia, Kenya, Rwanda, Russia, and Albania. Samaritan's Purse approached OCC with the proposition of expanding on a global scale, and the two charities merged in 1995.[1] Similar to other work done by Samaritan's Purse, OCC partners with local churches already ministering in local communities to children and their families. Samaritan's Purse was founded by Baptist minister Bob Pierce in 1970 to partner with local Evangelical churches worldwide to provide emergency supplies and doctors to areas experiencing war and natural catastrophes. Franklin Graham has directed the organization since Pierce's death in 1978. The organization exists both to provide humanitarian aid in disaster areas, and to proselytize for Evangelical Christianity.[2] The organization claims that as

1 "History of Operation Christmas Child," Samaritan's Purse United Kingdom, accessed November 9, 2018, https://samaritans-purse.org.uk/our-history.

2 Their mission statement reads, "Samaritan's Purse is a nondenominational evangelical Christian organization providing spiritual and physical aid to hurting people around the world. Since 1970, Samaritan's Purse has helped meet needs of people who are victims of war, poverty, natural disasters, disease, and

of 2024, they had delivered around 220 million shoeboxes.[3] It also claims to employ more than 540,000 global volunteers annually, 213,000 of which are located in the United States.[4] In 2009 OCC initiated a discipleship curriculum worldwide called The Greatest Journey, which follows up with the children who receive shoeboxes as a means of fulfilling OCC's evangelistic goals.[5]

To marshal that force of more than two hundred thousand American volunteers, OCC employs an array of aesthetic texts to persuade

---

famine with the purpose of sharing God's love through His Son, Jesus Christ. The organization serves the church worldwide to promote the Gospel of the Lord Jesus Christ." See "About Us", Samaritan's Purse, accessed August 31, 2016, https://www.samaritanspurse.org/our-ministry/about-us/. Franklin Graham himself asserts that the humanitarian aid exists for the purpose of supporting their proselytizing efforts. Graham writes in his autobiography, "I personally believe that when we respond as Christians to wars, famines, natural disasters, and other tragedies with food, medicine, and clothing, we earn a hearing for Christ. When people are down and out—whatever the circumstances—and we stop and help, they will listen to what we have to say. We have earned their respect. I want to take advantage of such opportunities to do everything I can to clearly, convincingly present Jesus Christ and his claims. . . . I would never take advantage of them for personal gain. But you better believe I will take advantage of every opportunity to reach them with the gospel message that can save them from the flames of hell." (Franklin Graham, *Rebel with a Cause: Finally Comfortable Being Graham; An Autobiography* [Thomas Nelson, Inc., 1995], 187).

3 "Fact Sheet—Operation Christmas Child," Samaritan's Purse, accessed March 16, 2024, https://tinyurl.com/39x5nvwy.

4 "Fact Sheet—Operation Christmas Child."

5 These goals represent a continuation of the ends articulated by Franklin Graham, reaching children and families "with the gospel message that can save them from the flames of hell." OCC notes that after receiving shoeboxes, "many children are invited back to participate in our discipleship program, The Greatest Journey. Through this 12-lesson course, which includes Bible stories and Scripture memorization, they learn how to follow Christ in their daily lives as they share Him with friends and family." OCC further claims, "Since 2009, more than 6.9 million children have reported decisions for Christ while taking The Greatest Journey. These children as well as those who hear the Gospel at shoebox outreach events share their faith with friends and family—who in turn disciple others." ("The Greatest Journey," Samaritan's Purse, accessed December 8, 2018, https://www.samaritanspurse.org/operation-christmas-child/the-greatest-journey/).

people to participate, and an extensive constellation of practices to accomplish their goals. OCC produces hundreds of these official texts each year. In addition, local churches and organizations create their own sets of aesthetic texts, and practices as a means of expressing the meaning they believe these communities should make from the sending of shoeboxes. These homemade pieces of material culture also represent a concrete means of persuading parishioners and community members to become colaborers in accomplishing OCC's goals. The practices enacted by participants reflect the communities in which the practices are performed.[6] For the purposes of analyzing the moral formation of these participants, the most popular types and pieces of material culture and aesthetic texts will be highlighted, along with the most common constellation of practices that result in the sending of Christmas shoeboxes.

THE AESTHETIC TEXTS OF OCC

The most common types of texts employed by OCC are books, pamphlets, posters, and videos.

Aesthetic Texts—*Miracle in a Shoebox*

The illustrated children's story *Miracle in a Shoebox: A Christmas Gift of Wonder* was written in 1995 by Franklin Graham with Estelle Condra and illustrated by Dilleen Marsh, shortly after Samaritan's Purse merged with OCC. The story highlights Jay Kelly in the United States, and Adnan Vacek in Bosnia, and the differences in their material and spiritual conditions. The book is a story of the spiritual impact that an OCC shoebox, sent by Jay, has on Adnan's family.

6 Regrettably, a thorough analysis of each of these community's texts and practices is not viable in this space.

In the story Jay learns of OCC and tells his mother about the ministry of sending shoeboxes.[7] Jay's mother affirms that the children in Bosnia had "nothing," admonishing Jay to "thank God for all our blessings."[8] Jay decides to use money he had set aside for Christmas to instead purchase presents for these children. Jay thinks of these children shivering in the snow and decides to buy them warm items such as hats and scarves.[9] His Sunday school teacher learns of his plans and asks him to speak to her class, and he agrees. Both his family and his church decide to join Jay in his efforts. In a conversation with his father, he states that he would want the fighting to stop if he lived in Bosnia. The father replies, "You know, Jay, we can't stop war with a shoe box. But we can pray that through the Christmas storybook that Samaritan's Purse is giving each child, they will find *real* peace—through Jesus Christ."[10] Jay includes a letter that indicates Jay is praying for whoever receives the box he is sending.

Across the globe in Bosnia, Adnan is living in the basement of a shelled building because his family's home has been burned. His father has been taken as a prisoner of war, which leaves him to live with his mother and sister. Describing Adnan's circumstances Graham writes, "Every day they hoped to hear that their father was alive. But there was no news—only the sounds of war and children crying."[11] Adnan learns of a ceasefire that will take place on Christmas Day. During the ceasefire he and other children receive gifts from OCC. While receiving these gifts a group of buses drive into the town square, releasing the prisoners of war, including Adnan's father. The book ends with a picture of the entire reunited family huddling around a candle, the father with a dark beard, the mother with a shawl over her head, likely meant to invoke images of the nativity. Huddled around this candle, the father tells the family that

7 Franklin Graham, with Estelle Condra, illustrated by Dilleen Marsh, *Miracle in a Shoe Box: A Christmas Gift of Wonder* (Thomas Nelson, 1995), 1.

8 Graham, *Miracle in a Shoe Box*, 1.

9 Graham, *Miracle in a Shoe Box*, 4.

10 Graham, *Miracle in a Shoe Box*, 9.

11 Graham, *Miracle in a Shoe Box*, 15.

he prayed in prison for God to show he cared. Because the father came home to hot food and presents for his children, he believes God answered that prayer, further noting, "Our friends in America have shown they care by sending these wonderful gifts. But God has given the greatest gift of all—His Son."[12] At the end of the book, the reader is given information regarding how they might participate in the program.

The Aesthetic Commitments of *Miracle in a Shoebox*

Early in the book, the American boy, Jay, is reminded by his mother that the Bosnian child they had witnessed in a video had "nothing," and that Jay and his family should "thank God for all our blessings."[13] This approach to the Bosnian's suffering by Jay's mother raises both theological and aesthetic questions. It raises the question of whether a lack of material possessions fundamentally equate to a lack of divine blessing, and whether the Bosnian family's want reveals that God's blessing was wholly, or perhaps substantially, absent from their lives.[14]

These assertions made by Jay's mother represent, at the very least, a passing narrative and subsequently a theological commitment to the notion that there is a correlation between a person's material possessions and the extent to which they are blessed by God.[15] Because this

---

12 Graham, *Miracle in a Shoe Box*, 29.

13 Graham, *Miracle in a Shoe Box*, 4.

14 It must be granted here that these are particularly rigorous questions to be asking of a children's story. However, the story is written in such a way that the elders in the story, and eventually the children as well, are framed as articulating an approach to these questions that is framed normatively by its authors, both ethically and theologically. Additionally, on a more fundamental level we must ask whether this assertion is even true. Would actual Bosnian families livening in similar circumstances have agreed with Jay's mother? There is no way of knowing for sure; however, Jay's mother's description of their circumstances skews toward the hyperbolic as a means of heightening the experience of significance associated with participation in the sending of shoeboxes.

15 Though not clearly articulated, unspoken is the supposition that the character's and thus the author's theological approach to the relationship between

is a commitment that relates to material objects, this also represents the character's and in this case the author's aesthetic commitments. Thus when Jay commits to buying warm hats and scarves in order to pack them in the shoebox and send them to these children, he believes he is sharing God's blessings with his Bosnian counterpart, because each object essentially represents an instantiation of divine blessing.

The description of the relationship between material possessions and divine blessings articulated in the book represents a snapshot of Graham's and OCC's aesthetic commitments, the manner in which their own affections and dispositions have been formed. Aesthetic commitments are not necessarily doctrinal commitments. Doctrine represents a rational articulation of spiritual beliefs, propositions, or commitments. Aesthetic commitments are rooted in one's affections and dispositions. As such they are not fundamentally rational. Instead these aesthetic commitments represent ways of perceiving that have been formed by aesthetic processes. *Miracle in a Shoebox* intimates a disposition that experiences material possessions as evidence of Divine blessing in the life of Christians. This aesthetic and narrative commitment, and the disposition it funds, then shapes the Christian's relationship to, their perception of, and their affection for material objects and the physical world.[16]

These perceptions result in at least two outcomes. First, the collection or loss of material possessions becomes affectively tied to the perceived experience of divine blessing. If one were to lose a significant portion of their material possessions, one would experience that loss, at the very least, as evidence of a relational distance from God. Following this thread of reasoning, one might also expect this type of loss to signify an experience of divine judgment. Correspondingly,

---

material possessions and divine blessings is a faithful articulation of the biblical witness as it relates to material possessions.

16 Interestingly, these aesthetic commitments also represent, or perhaps instantiate, a particular set of theological or doctrinal commitments. They represent a particular understanding of and commitment to an understanding of how God acts in people's lives. These aesthetic commitments frame a particular understanding of the meaning of divine/human interactions.

an increase of one's material possessions would be experienced not only as the bulwarking of one's comfort and security; it would also represent an affective source of existential well-being as it is evidence of divine favor.[17]

Second, and perhaps ironically, the physical becomes a doorway to the spiritual. While evangelism and a spiritually framed salvation remains the telos for OCC, it embraces the value of material possessions to specifically serve those ends. However, these material possessions are not afforded a fundamental value. In other words, they do not represent a good unto themselves. They become undifferentiated material representations or symbols of divine blessing, love, and grace. Put simply, the material objects packed in shoeboxes are of secondary importance to their fundamentally spiritual telos. Even as material items are packed into shoeboxes and sent into the world as instantiations of divine love, the significance of the box's materiality is de-emphasized, particularly in light of a salvation that also de-emphasizes the importance of materiality. This speaks to the notion of the good embodied in the practices of OCC. The telos, as framed here, is one that generally discounts the theological value of creation as a good unto itself. Thus, by extension, the physical experiences of the people created in the image of God are also discounted as a fundamental good. Instead, OCC steers its participants toward a telos that locates the good almost entirely within a divine future beyond the materiality of creation. Both outcomes highlight an approach to the material, and subsequently to embodiment, that de-emphasizes the significance of the physical world and favors an aesthetic and theological account of materiality and the body that exists to serve exclusively spiritual ends. The practices are then organized accordingly.[18]

---

17 This also speaks to Bourdieu's social account of the formation of taste (the formation of one's affections and dispositions), as that individual's sense of the social import of any particular material object is read through a divine sociality in addition to being read through the lens of social distinction.

18 We must note that these themes are not unique to *Miracle in a Shoebox*. This disposition is also embedded in the videos produced by OCC.

If the aesthetic texts of OCC instantiate a disposition that ascribes value to the material and to creation in terms of the spiritual outcomes it facilitates, and if a community's practices represent a dramatic rendering of their aesthetic commitments and dispositions, then OCC's practices are framed in light of these commitments. Here, the aesthetic commitments in OCC's aesthetic texts become embodied in participant's dramatic actions, or practices.

Aesthetic Texts—Online Videos

The other most common aesthetic text employed as a means of persuading people to participate are videos. OCC has produced hundreds of videos through the years, from short commercial-length clips to some that run half an hour or more. These videos are downloadable and are intended to be shared during worship services and community gatherings. There are several themes that are repeated in these types of videos. Among them is the notion that when sending a shoe box, one is not just sending a gift, one is sending love.[19] The videos also often emphasize that the receiving of these gifts is the first time many of these children have received a present, particularly at Christmas, emphasizing the joy, smiles, and childlike silliness that accompanies the opening of these presents.[20]

The other common type of video produced by OCC is the personal testimony video. The most common video subjects are people outside of the United States who had received shoeboxes as children and believe their lives were affected positively by these gifts. These stories also tend to touch on similar notes in their narratives. Often the person sharing their story describes an experience of not feeling loved, and not owning any items they could call their own. Upon receiving the shoebox from OCC they express deep gratitude and

19 See "How Shoeboxes Spread Good News and Great Joy," Samaritan's Purse, accessed August 30, 2016, http://video.samaritanspurse.org/how-shoeboxes-spread-good-news-and-great-joy-57/.

20 See "Bringing Light to Cameroon," Samaritan's Purse, accessed December 19, 2024, https://video.samaritanspurse.org/bringing-light-to-cameroon-2/.

believe that the gift they received simultaneously introduced them to the notion that they were loved by God, and often marked the beginning of their own Christian discipleship.[21] These are uniform stories of hope found through the gift of the shoeboxes.

Both types of videos highlight that the physicality of the shoeboxes affectively persuades their senders and recipients to follow Christ. An unnamed African pastor in one of the videos asserts, "A gift carries a stronger message. That is the gospel in action."[22] Advocating for the viewer's participation in the program evangelist Louie Giglio asserts, "There are children's lives around the world right now that are linked to our story and we're linked to their story through what Samaritan's Purse and Operation Christmas Child makes reality."[23] He notes further, "There's a real story on the other end of that box, so why wouldn't you want to be part of a story like this?"[24] Another video opens with a black and white image of a sad-looking animated child. Once he receives his present from OCC, his world becomes colorized and alive. The narrator indicates that his world was transformed by the love of Jesus.[25] These videos employ music, videos of children receiving gifts, and narratives framing these scenes in the experiential and theological terms described. In doing so, they endeavor to stir the emotions of the viewer as a means of encouraging

---

21 See "Livia's Shoebox Story," http://video.samaritanspurse.org/livias-shoebox-story/, "Nanor's Shoebox Story," https://video.samaritanspurse.org/nanors-shoebox-story/, https://video.samaritanspurse.org/teds-story/, https://video.samaritanspurse.org/irinas-story/. The former orphan in this video was told by someone from Samaritan's purse that there was a God and that God wanted to adopt her, which she cites as every orphan's dream; and "Zarina's Story," http://video.samaritanspurse.org/full-circle-zarina/.

22 "Shoeboxes for Every Tribe, Tongue and Nation!," Samaritan's Purse, accessed August 30, 2016, http://video.samaritanspurse.org/oc-130105-occ-connect-international-welcome-st_mix-m4v/.

23 "From Your Church to the World through OCC," Samaritan's Purse, accessed August 30, 2016, http://video.samaritanspurse.org/from-your-church-to-the-world-through-occ/.

24 "From Your Church to the World through OCC."

25 "How Shoeboxes Spread News and Great Joy," Samaritan's Purse, accessed August 30, 2016, http://video.samaritanspurse.org/oc-150101d-occ-main-report-animation-only-web-mix-m4v/.

their participation in OCC. Each of these types of videos intends to persuade its viewer toward a particular set of embodied actions: that is, the filling and shipping of shoeboxes to children like those presented in these videos. The creators of these videos are endeavoring to accomplish that end by appealing to and ultimately shaping the viewer's affections and imagination.

OCC Videos and the Formation of Affections

In the following examples, participants personally cite the formational effect of the videos on both their participation in the practices of OCC and on their affections and imagination. In addition, they describe how they understand the performance of those practices to enact a vision of faithful Christian discipleship. The first is a woman named Karen Dickinson from Atlanta Bible Church in Atlanta, Michigan. In describing a part of her motivation for packing shoeboxes she states, "All you need to do is see a couple of these videos about the OCC and your heart will be there with them. You see the joy on these kid's faces who may have never had anything at all for Christmas and it is just wonderful."[26] The second is Donna Cox from First MB Church in Wichita, Kansas. She describes her interactions with both Samaritan Purse's magazine and its online videos. She and her husband David organized a neighborhood packing party after reading about the idea in a magazine published by OCC and Samaritan's Purse. Of the videos produced by OCC she says, "Most people have now looked at the videos online and have seen those children when they get those boxes. It breaks my heart to see children who know nothing about Jesus or love or maybe even parents or have never received a gift."[27] She goes on to say, "People want to do good. They just have to have direction, and it's just so exciting

26 "Operation Christmas Child Packing Party, Atlanta Bible Church", YouTube, November 15, 2016, accessed October 10, 2017, https://www.youtube.com/watch?v=soieh3cL7hc, 1:28.

27 "Operation Christmas Child Neighborhood Packing Party!," YouTube, November 2, 2016, accessed October 10, 2017, https://www.youtube.com/watch?v=o1jBqvDCESw, 1:15.

to think that in this neighborhood we can make a difference clear around the world."[28] For Mrs. Cox, the videos provided at least a part of that direction.[29]

In both instances the influence of the videos produced by OCC on the imagination and actions of these two participants is clear. Both articulate an affinity for the narrative instantiated in OCC's videos, particularly as it relates to the happiness and joy experienced by those receiving shoeboxes. Both emphasize their enjoyment of witnessing the recipient's joy. Both articulate a desire to be a part of participating in the creation of the good represented by the shoebox recipient's joy. Participants then enact that particular narrative as they partake in the packing and sending of shoeboxes to these children.[30]

However, there is a conundrum here whether these participants are simply performing narratives that were already embedded in their dispositions or whether OCC's aesthetic texts created these affections. Even if OCC's aesthetic texts are directing the enactment of narratives the participant is already disposed to perform, the texts still contribute to the participant's continued formation. These aesthetic texts then represent more than just visual cues; they represent something like a script that participants see themselves performing. The texts also aid in the formation of the emotional meaning attributed to these performances. For the participants described here, the aesthetic texts of OCC contribute to the ongoing formation of already-formed affections that fund their performance of OCC practices. Therefore, these aesthetic texts are contributing to the continued formation of the participant's dispositions toward a particular formational end.

---

28 "Operation Christmas Child Neighborhood Packing Party!," 1:51.

29 In addition to these two, there are many across the multitude of videos posted to You Tube that do not directly mention the relationship of OCC's videos to their actions, but refer to the smiling faces of those who receive an OCC shoebox. It seems reasonable to believe that those who mention the children's smiles have seen OCC's videos and have had their imaginations and affections formed by the affective power of that portion of OCC's narrative.

30 We must note that there are of course myriad other narratives being performed by each of these participants.

THE PRACTICES OF OCC

As with any large organization or institution OCC animates both official and unofficial practices among its participants. OCC provides guidelines for participants and links to opportunities to participate in official practices. They also offer suggestions and ideas for organizing practices that can be framed as unofficial. The most essential of the official practices is shopping for the shoeboxes themselves. OCC provides specific instructions regarding the types of items that should be included. The individual or group is instructed to start with a shoebox, or something of a similar size, and then choose the recipient's gender and age range (two to four, five to nine, or ten to fourteen are OCC's chosen age brackets). OCC suggests that the sender "select a quality 'wow' toy such as a doll, soccer ball with pump, or stuffed animal. Then add other fun toys, hygiene items, and school supplies."[31] The website also suggests that the most important part of the process is prayer for the recipient of the box.[32]

Other official practices listed by OCC fall under the category of volunteering. Because the boxes are intended to be delivered at Christmas, they are officially collected at distribution centers during the second week in November every year. The practices are then largely shipping related: consolidating and packing the shoeboxes

31 "How to Pack a Shoebox," Samaritan's Purse, accessed August 31, 2016, https://www.samaritanspurse.org/operation-christmas-child/pack-a-shoebox/.

32 These practices associated with sending the shoeboxes then can be broken up into several parts: the practice of shopping for the items, the practices associated with packing and shipping the items, and the practice of praying for the recipient of the shoebox. One could include here the general practices and customs of the shopper, including the customs associated with their store of choice, the driving of the routes the shopper might take to the store, the music or radio programming he may enjoy on the way to the store, the type of food that is consumed either on the way to or at the store or mall, and the personal or familial customs associated with the consumption of meals or snacks. Thus, it must be noted that any official practice can, and perhaps must, be nested within the larger constellation of rituals and unofficial practices that constitute an individual's routine.

into larger containers that can then be shipped worldwide. OCC also seeks year-round help from other types of volunteers, including administrative support, church relations, community relations, logistics, media relations, prayer mobilization, and student relations.[33]

OCC suggests many unofficial practices, or practices not directly sanctioned by OCC. The performance of these practices relies on the individual or group organizing them. Among the unofficial practices suggested by OCC are hosting packing parties and raising funds for OCC. Other unofficial practices are creatively constructed among local communities such as viewing videos during worship services and church services created to consecrate and celebrate boxes before and after they are shipped.[34] Many people also create homemade toys and crafts specifically to be shipped for OCC, and see this as a personal ministry. There are dozens of Pinterest pages dedicated to this set of practices.[35] These are all practices manifested at a grassroots level and are full of creativity and imaginative energy.

In each of these sets of practices, the participants are layering their performed meaning on top of the foundation of OCC's official practices. Both official and unofficial practices are important

33 "Volunteer Year Round with Operation Christmas Child," Samaritan's Purse, accessed August 31, 2016. https://www.samaritanspurse.org/operation-christmas-child/volunteer-year-round/.

34 For examples of both types of liturgies see "First Presbyterian Church—Operation Christmas Child 2015," November 18, 2015, https://www.youtube.com/watch?v=lji8Pay5Ve4 (First Presbyterian Church in Columbus, GA); Shiloh Baptist Church—Operation Christmas Child Shoebox Dedication 2013," November 26, 2013, https://www.youtube.com/watch?v=27mQ94j5GAE (Shiloh Baptist Church in Bridgeport, IL); "Operation Christmas Child Dedication," November 13, 2011, https://www.youtube.com/watch?v=Mw8FfoRl-Is (Ross Baptist Church in Windsor, NC); "NPCUCC Sunday Service Operation Christmas Child 11 05 2017," November 5, 2017, https://www.youtube.com/watch?v=gGrtpE37Ocg (North Port Community United Church of Christ in North Port, FL), and "Operation Christmas Child—River Run Christian Church," October 26, 2008, https://www.youtube.com/watch?v=CXVpiIngJ3A (River Run Christian Church in Melbourne, FL).

35 As an example, Savanah Summerfield, "things to make for Operation christmas child" [*sic*], Pinterest, https://www.pinterest.com/savanahsummerfi/things-to-make-for-operation-christmas-child/

because the performance of both sets of practices underwrite the individual's, and by extension the community's, moral formation. In both official and unofficial practices, OCC participants dramatically embody parts of the vision of the good life instantiated in its aesthetic texts. In that way the actions of the participants represent a dramatic rendering, or an enactment, of the aesthetic and ethical commitments embedded in those texts.[36]

To follow the formational strand between aesthetic text and formation the practice of packing shoeboxes will offer a window into understanding the narratives embedded in the practice and the manner in which those narratives are performed. It will also offer a window into the manner in which the practice engages the participants' senses and the social and cultural lenses employed by the participants as a means of making sense of these practices. It will also allow for the consideration of whether these texts and practices (and practices as texts) may be working to forming the imaginations, dispositions, and the subsequent practices of its participants.

Packing Shoeboxes: Practices

Before accounting for the narratives enacted in the packing of shoeboxes, there are several micropractices upon which the practice of shoebox packing is constructed. First, the practices associated with shopping: transportation to and from a store, the walking, browsing,

36 Of note, the interlacing of practices in terms of their effects on the potential moral formation of both individuals and communities frames them within the terms of virtue ethic discourse. These notions of official and unofficial practices can be seen as operating within a MacIntyrian framework. He frames practices as "any coherent and complex form of socially established cooperative human activity through which goods internal to that form of activity are realized in the course of trying to achieve those standards of excellence which are appropriate to, and partially definitive of, that form of activity, with the result that human powers to achieve excellence, and human conceptions of the ends and good involved, are systemically extended"(MacIntyre, *After Virtue*, 187). Within this framework these practices are initiated and sustained by institutions and enact its ideals of the good life (194).

and consumer-based decision-making that are a part of choosing the best product for the purchaser's intended purposes. Also included is the forethought and imagination necessary that is part of the process of choosing the best presents. If the participant purchases the items to be packed in the shoebox at an online retailer, a different set of practices associated with computer use, online shopping, and social media would come into play. Once the shopping is complete, there are the practices associated with packing the shoebox. These practices would depend on the social setting of the packing. An individual packing a shoebox by themselves would embody an entirely different set of practices than an individual packing a shoebox or shoeboxes with one's family, or at packing parties.[37] However, each of these sets of practices represent the enactment of particular narratives embedded in the aesthetic texts of OCC.

Packing Shoeboxes: Narratives

There are narratives that the various entities associated with the packing of boxes (Samaritan's Purse, participating churches, and individuals) believe they are enacting, and there are also narratives they are unaware they are enacting. The practices directly associated with OCC fall under the larger Samaritan's Purse organization. As the name suggests, it frames its work under the overarching narrative of Jesus's parable of the good Samaritan.[38] OCC's website writes, "After sharing the story of the Good Samaritan, Jesus said 'Go and do likewise.' That is the mission of Samaritan's Purse—to follow the example of Christ by helping those in need and proclaiming the hope of the Gospel."[39] Thus Samaritan's Purse frames its entire

---

37 OCC even offers a checklist to help organize a successful packing party. "Customize Your Packing Party," https://www.samaritanspurse.org/operation-christmas-child/packing-parties/, Samaritan's Purse, accessed March 7, 2017.

38 See Luke 10:25–37.

39 "About Us," https://www.samaritanspurse.org/our-ministry/about-us/, Samaritan's Purse, accessed March 7, 2017.

ministry as the analogical imitation of the healing acts performed by the Samaritan in the Gospel of Luke.[40]

In addition, both Samaritan's Purse and OCC understand themselves as enacting a complementary scriptural narrative. Each frames its purpose in terms of evangelism and discipleship. Thus, they indicate that they believe they are enacting what is in Evangelical parlance often called The Great Commission, Christ's imperative to the church to preach the gospel to the whole world.[41] These two narratives represent what can be described as Samaritan Purse's and OCC's primary telos. In addition, OCC also instantiates a more devotionally rooted narrative that interlaces the collection of the goods shipped in the shoeboxes with the divine love instantiated in the Gospel narratives and embodied in the life of Jesus. In short, the items in the shoebox are intended to convey the message that through Jesus Christ, God loves the recipient of that box in a manner specific to the Gospel narratives. These become the central narratives OCC and Samaritan's Purse use to shape the dispositions, imaginations, and practices of OCC participants. Interestingly, churches build on these official narratives and add narratives of their own they believe they are enacting.

---

40 I must note that Samaritan's Purse as an organization does not provide a clear articulation of which aspects of the good Samaritan narrative they are enacting. One of the key points in the narrative is that the one serving to facilitate the healing of the injured traveler was himself a member of a community who would likely have been marginalized by each of the other characters in the story. Samaritan's Purse and OCC do not emphasize that their participant's actions represent that portion of the narrative. Instead, they seem to highlight simply the imitation of the service to the one who is injured.

41 The text of this imperative is recorded in Matt 28:18-20: "Jesus came up and spoke to them, saying, 'All authority has been given to Me in heaven and on earth. Go therefore and **make disciples of all the nations**, baptizing them in the name of the Father and the Son and the Holy Spirit, teaching them to observe all that I commanded you; and lo, I am with you always, even to the end of the age'" (NKJV). As an example see "The Greatest Journey" https://www.samaritanspurse.org/operation-christmas-child/the-greatest-journey/, Samaritan's Purse, accessed March 7, 2017.

When individuals, churches, and organizations describe the narratives that undergird the localized practices associated with packing shoeboxes, there is a general conformity with the broad narratives articulated and inferred by Samaritan's Purse and OCC. However other narratives that do not originate in the official OCC narratives find their way into the narratives faith communities and their individual members believe they are enacting in the practices associated with OCC.[42] Among the narratives that consistently arise in individual's accounts of the packing and shipping shoeboxes is that these practices are fundamentally pleasurable, gratifying, and fun. These experiences are associated with the social aspects of packing. Often, accounts of packing shoeboxes recall sharing time with friends and family. Because the gifts packed for OCC are distributed at Christmas, these gatherings often take the general form of Christmas parties, with Christmas music, food, and games. This then becomes a complex web of narratives that also enact scriptural imperatives relating to hospitality, Jesus's invocation that Christians are to care for "the least of these" in the Gospel of Matthew,[43] narratives directly related to the birth of Jesus, and the notions of self-gifting love that are interspersed throughout the Gospel narrative. The embedded narratives are enacted alongside cultural narratives regarding the performance of hospitality, gender roles, practices that enact both family and cultural Christmas traditions, and the social dynamics specific to gatherings. Layered on those narratives are the social and personally affective experiences American popular culture often associates with Christmas (nostalgia, joy, melancholy, loneliness,

42 For example see below. These offer various account of the types of stories and blogs relating to specific experiences associated with OCC: Jaime Erickson, "Operation Christmas Child Packing Party," *The Unlikely Homeschool* (blog), September, 2012, http://www.theunlikelyhomeschool.com/2012/09/operation-christmas-child-packing-party.html and Jake Flannick, "Volunteers Hold Operation Christmas Child Packing Party," *Citizen Times*, November 25, 2016, http://www.citizen-times.com/story/life/2016/11/25/volunteers-hold-operation-christmas-child-packing-party/93234340/.

43 See Matt 25:31–46.

hope). The web of narratives is complex when the participant packs a shoebox. The participant's actions then reveal themselves as nuanced performances of these narratives, emphasizing particular and personal combinations of narratives with their performance.

Packing Shoeboxes: Performances

Interestingly, the performances that grow out of these narratives may seem to lack the complexity of the web of narratives being performed. This is because, as it relates to the packing of shoeboxes, the specifics of their performances share a good deal of consistency. Aside from the choice of the items placed in the box, and the choice of the gender of the box's recipient, the performance of filling a shoe box does not allow for significant amounts of variation.[44] However, the simplicity and consistency of the performance does not negate the complexity of the narratives that fund that performance. Among the most common narratives cited by those sharing in these performances is the scriptural and perhaps cultural narrative that emphasizes the importance of sharing, particularly with those with fewer possessions

44 Interestingly, the general consistency and repeatability of the practices associated with the packing of shoeboxes become something of its own Christian ritual for some. The study of the ritualization of this packing and its potential evolution into something like its own type of liturgy would make for compelling further study. There are already those who include "countdown celebrations," which are largely Free Church liturgies designed to persuade people to participate in the practices of OCC, and provide devotional, theological and ritualistic support for these practices, as a part of their yearly Christmas tradition. See Michelle McConnaha, "Church Hosts Operation Christmas Child Countdown Event," *Ravalli Republic*, October 19, 2016, http://ravallirepublic.com/news/local/article_1767549a-965f-11e6-aac9-3731e0e4ba37.html, Journey Baptist Church, "Operation Christmas Child—Countdown Event," October 7, 2016, Vimeo, https://vimeo.com/186033970, Christ Church, "Special Speaker: Operation Christmas Child Countdown Event," October 29, 2014, Vimeo, https://vimeo.com/110402216, Calvary Chapel Chico, "Operation Christmas Child Launch 2015," YouTube, October 23, 2015, https://www.youtube.com/watch?v=1QYu29Fr0P8, and Samaritan's Purse, "Operation Christmas Child Celebration in Charlotte," YouTube, December 7, 2016, https://www.youtube.com/watch?time_continue=4&v=2DyKVRsJk5s.

than the one doing the sharing.[45] This is often framed colloquially as "giving back." Another narrative being performed is that of materially instantiating divine love in the shoebox.[46] This narrative often frames the sender as uniquely sharing the love of God with the shoebox's recipient. It simultaneously frames the recipient as one who has experienced no, or a particularly meager sense, of divine or familial love in their local and social context prior to receiving the shoebox. In addition, there is also the performance of a narrative that directly associates material possessions with well-being, and a narrative of self-improvement. Unspoken within this self-improvement narrative is the notion that the filling of shoeboxes is as much about the growth, fulfillment, and the benefits received by the one filling and sending the box as it is about sharing the gospel and beneficial material resources with a child in poverty.

Framed within an aesthetic matrix, the performances of these narratives become their own aesthetic texts to be read and affectively imbibed by others within the community of those present. Performed narratives are themselves aesthetic texts. They are the embodied performances of these narrative webs and are thus available to the senses of others. These performances carry the same affective weight as any other narrative and thus shape the participant's imaginations, dispositions, and actions—be they written or enacted, fictional or nonfictional. Interestingly, this means that aesthetic texts carry the potential to doubly influence the ethics and practices of a community, both in that community's immediate experience of affectivity, and through the embodied affective appeal as the community embraces and enacts many of the narratives performed in these culturally constructed aesthetic texts. Additionally, the performed narratives further shape the practices, dispositions, and imaginations of participants to the extent that they provide the impetus for the creation

45 See Flannick, "Volunteers Hold Operation Christmas Child."

46 Flannick, "Volunteers Hold Operation Christmas Child." In the article referenced a North Carolina woman states, "Children need to know they are loved." The flip side of this narrative frames its performance as one of Christian and perhaps even American exceptionalism.

of new and referential pieces of material culture that themselves instantiate and memorialize these narratives, strengthening the reinforcing circle.

So then, if a person's disposition and imagination is constructed by means of narrative processes, and those processes operate by means of that person's senses, then those who participate in the practices of OCC experience something of this formation. This means these practices operate to form its participants morally and devotionally. They work to form the dispositions and imaginations of its participants and fund the formation of practices rooted in the affections formed out of these dispositions. In short, OCC's aesthetic texts and material culture contribute to the formation of virtue in its participants.

THE RELATION OF THE AESTHETIC TO OCC PRACTICES

There is a line between the practices of particular OCC participants and their own aesthetic commitments, particularly as they are rooted in OCC's aesthetic texts and material culture.[47] In order to describe the manner in which the aesthetic commitments of these participants become embodied through dramatic action, a return to the two axes of embodiment and performance on the one hand, and meaning making and narrative on the other, will prove helpful to articulate the overlap between the aesthetic and the dramatic. In

47 A relevant line of exploration that will not be included in this study would be an attempt to articulate a relationship between the aesthetic and dramatic (texts and practices), framed in both conceptual and causal terms. If dramatic discourse is interlaced with and constructed on aesthetic discourse, and both require the engagement of similar bodily processes to participate in that discourse, the relationship between the two must be understood to be closely related, conceptually. However, in addition, one must understand the circular causal relationship between the two. The aesthetic both shapes and is shaped by the dramatic. Each is formed by, and then forms the other over time. Practices are formed around and in relation to aesthetic texts, and those practices shape the imagination and consequently inspire fresh aesthetic texts.

order to describe how these commitments are enacted in the lives of these participants, a return to the self-representations of these practices as they are enacted and documented, both individually and in the lives of churches and communities, will prove fruitful as well.

Embodiment and Performance

The first representative example as it relates to describing the relationship between aesthetics and the practices associated with OCC is a video produced by Arcadia Friend's Community Church (AFCC) in Arcadia, California. The video includes a text displayed between images of church members and others packing shoeboxes and playing and dancing together. Over the sounds of the song "Christmas This Year" by artists TobyMac and Leigh Nash, the text affirms that the shoeboxes sent by those seen in the video are sent "to needy children all over the world."[48] In addition the video suggests or requests, "Christmas this year, share God's love with shoebox gifts. Celebrate the greatest gift of all."[49] This represents a rearticulation of OCC's notion that a shoebox represents an instantiation of the love of God. The practices of AFCC (dramatized in their video) enact the aesthetic commitments and dispositions articulated in OCC's aesthetic texts and material culture. The material shoeboxes sent by AFCC through OCC represent the church's efforts to promote the recipient's and the participant's experience of the good life and Christian discipleship consistent with OCC's envisioning of each.

A further example of this relationship between AFCC's enactment of the aesthetic commitments embedded in OCC's aesthetic texts can be seen near the end of this video. The video's creator juxtaposes dancing children attending AFCC's packing party with the stock footage produced by Samaritan's Purse of shoebox recipients dancing

48 "Operation Christmas Child Packing Party 2014 at Arcadia Friends Community Church," November 16, 2014, YouTube, https://www.youtube.com/watch?v=UjCdaK4iTEA, 2:01.

49 Flannick, "Volunteers Hold Operation Christmas Child," 2:05.

upon receiving a Christmas shoebox from OCC. Conspicuous in this juxtaposition is the difference in the physical conditions that surround each set of children. The children of AFCC are packing material goods that could be read as excess resources made available for this program. The children receiving shoeboxes are filmed in tattered clothes, often with no shoes, in churches and houses with dirt floors. These differences serve to heighten the sentimental effect of these comparisons and are thus vital to the video's ability to affectively engage its viewer. However, the differences do not (and because it is rooted in difference cannot) represent the crux of the analogy being drawn by the video's creator.[50] The analogy is rooted in the joy of both sets of children. They are affectively (and rightly) arguing for a common humanity between those who send and those who receive shoeboxes. However, the aesthetic commitment that minimizes the importance of materiality of the children's bodies allows the vast social and economic differences to be set aside so that the emotional experience of joy is what the children hold in common, particularly as it relates to receiving presents which instantiate the love of God on Christmas. AFCC has an aesthetic commitment to a materiality that values the potential to serve spiritual ends that creates a community of individuals disposed to perceive the children's poverty and their bodily conditions in largely spiritual terms. It thus creates a sense of Christian discipleship, and a Christian disciple who privileges a concern for and subsequently a provision for the child's perceived spiritual needs. However, it also creates a disciple not disposed to perceive the betterment of the child's material conditions as a good in itself, particularly as that betterment is rooted in Christian practices.

Another example of the enactment of the aesthetic commitments embedded in OCC's aesthetic texts can be seen in the video posted by Atlanta Bible Church (ABC). In the video, James Larsen, the producer and narrator of the video and the teenage son of the church's

50 The video's creator also may be drawing on a common American Protestant/Evangelical narrative that associates spiritual poverty with material poverty.

pastor, Ron Larsen, declares, "When you look at these kid's faces, when they receive their boxes, they are so priceless, full of joy. And bringing hope into these places where there is no hope at all is an incredible thing to do."[51] He goes on to state later in the video, "These kids, they have no hope. They have nothing to look forward to, but that's where the gospel comes in. They have eternal life through Jesus Christ, and it makes such an impact on their lives when they see the love of God. And that seriously is the most amazing thing about Operation Christmas Child."[52] These descriptions of his and the church's motivations for participating in OCC articulate the aesthetic roots of their actions. Larsen argues that the gospel message, in terms of the eternal life the child receives through faith in Jesus, is what ultimately changes the boxes recipient's lives for the better. The material and bodily conditions of the children are not articulated here as a motivating factor in Larsen's participation. Here, the rescue of the soul is privileged over the rescue of the body. Thus, Larsen's descriptions of his and the church's reasons for participation in OCC represent their aesthetic commitments to materiality.[53]

This aesthetic commitment of ABC to OCC affects the church's practical and devotional practices throughout the year. The video

51 "Operation Christmas Child—2017 Packing Party," YouTube, November 15, 2017, accessed December 30, 2017, https://www.youtube.com/watch?v=dbkadtbuQbM, 1:21.

52 "Operation Christmas Child—2017 Packing Party," 3:09.

53 To be clear, there is no suggestion that Samaritan's Purse is entirely unconcerned with the physical state of the children in these videos. Indeed, the primary ministry of Samaritan's Purse is disaster relief, that is, the preservation of life and the physical restoration of communities. As it states on its website, "We specialize in meeting critical needs for victims of conflict, disaster, famine, and epidemics throughout the world, often working through ministry partners on the ground. We provide food, water, shelter, medicine, and other assistance in the Name of Jesus Christ." ("International Crisis Response," Samaritan's Purse, accessed January 4, 2018, https://www.samaritanspurse.org/what-we-do/international-crisis-response/). Instead, we must note that these broader considerations are not generally used as the primary frame in their aesthetic texts, and thus they are not a part of the practices that grow out of those aesthetic texts.

includes members and the pastor stating that they set aside bins outside the church where parishioners store items for OCC.[54] The packing of shoeboxes seems to have found a home in the affections and imagination of the church, and as such has manifested and embedded itself in their practices. In addition, the practices associated with OCC seem to have become a part of the church's expression of discipleship and a teleological expression of their understanding of the good life to be embodied by the church.[55] These practices represent how these particular sets of participants understand the bodies of others, in this case the bodies of those who receive shoeboxes. But the formation does not stop there; OCC's practices also shape and express the manner in which participants frame and understand their own bodies.

A video created by Christchurch Evangelical Covenant Church (CECC) in Portland, Maine poses the question, "What does it take to pack 600 shoeboxes in 90 minutes?"[56] The video employs editing tools to condense the entire packing process down to around three minutes while an instrumental version of the song "Good King Wenceslas" plays in the background.[57] The video ends with the church's answer

---

54 See "Operation Christmas Child 2017 Packing Party," YouTube, November 15, 2017, https://www.youtube.com/watch?v=dbkadtbuQbM, 2:07 and 2:24

55 Interestingly, some of the church members who participate in this shopping seem to take pleasure in the rituals and practices associated with acquiring these material objects. This represents an intriguing irony given the aesthetic commitments to materiality they are enacting. This speaks to the extent to which humanity is embedded in and dependent upon the materiality of the world. This is true even for those intent on articulating a largely spiritual meaning for that embeddedness. This also speaks to the cross currents of aesthetic formation where affections, dispositions, and practices are being pulled toward competing teloi.

56 Christchurch Portland Maine, "600 Shoeboxes in 90 Minutes! An Operation Christmas Child Packing Party," YouTube, November 16, 2015, https://www.youtube.com/watch?v=nWH7Cw50LmE, 0:05.

57 The choice of song here is entirely appropriate. A further conversation regarding the juxtaposition of the song's narrative alongside the church's practices in this instance might prove both fascinating and fruitful.

to the question it posed at its opening, writing, "What does it take? It takes God's love working through us!"[58]

"God's love working through us" and other ambiguous justifications for packing shoeboxes allows a useful question to be raised: whether God's love is most manifest in the shoebox and its contents or in the actions of those packing them. If the shoeboxes are best understood by those who pack them as instantiations of divine love that privilege a spiritual telos, then it would follow that they also represent particular instantiations of "God's love working through us." This represents an aesthetic commitment that (as noted) does not ascribe a fundamental value to the particulars packed in the shoeboxes. Subsequently there is not a fundamental value to the physical bodies who pack them and the work it takes to pack. The significance is placed on the instantiation of divine love.[59]

The video from CECC highlights participants' dispositions as they relate to general bodily processes. The emphasis is on the divine love represented by a packed shoebox. Deemphasized are the bodily actions necessary for its packing, and necessary for creating the space and environment for packing (decorating, setting up tables and packing stations, driving, shopping, and socializing to name but a few). This approach represents aesthetic commitments as they relate to the body that carry over from the participant's general aesthetic commitments to materiality. The participants are thus drawn toward a telos, a notion of the good life, and authentic Christian discipleship that privileges spiritual ends over material ones, spiritual process over bodily processes. This forms the participant's perceptions, imaginations, and understanding of what is being accomplished through their work, and what constitutes authentic instantiations and embodiments of divine love. They aesthetically form the very

58 Christchurch Portland Maine, "600 Shoeboxes in 90 Minutes!," 3:16.

59 To borrow Lyotard's phraseology, the significance is assigned to the discreet unit of divine affection as opposed to the gestus of the body necessary to produce that discreet unit.

perceptions of what constitutes the proper form of authentic Christian discipleship.

Meaning Making and Narrative

Packing shoeboxes also represents projects of meaning making. In fact, the entire intent behind packing a shoebox is to project meaning into the life of its recipient. However, the project also enacts particular meanings and aesthetic commitments by those doing the packing.

The Mommy Archives is the project of a woman named Jessica from Fort Worth, Texas. She intends the vlog to be "a digital resource of information, entertainment, and community for modern women and moms."[60] In a video from November of 2017, Jessica films herself, her two daughters, and her husband shopping for shoebox items in a Target store. Jessica's husband explains to their eldest daughter, who appears to be in early childhood, that they are buying items for shoeboxes because "we want them [the recipients of the boxes] to know about Jesus."[61] Once the shopping is complete, the rest of the video is spent meticulously describing every item purchased, restating the reasons why they were purchased, and showing the process of packing the shoeboxes. Toward the end of the video she invites her viewers, "Let me know what you guys are doing this holiday season to give back."[62] Interestingly, this provides a second meaning ascribed to the practices enacted in the video. Jessica and her family are sending shoeboxes both to project the story of Jesus/the gospel into the world and to "give back." These motivations represent differently rooted, perhaps even competing projects of meaning making.

---

60 "About," *The Mommy Archives*, accessed January 1, 2018, http://www.themommyarchives.com/about-me/.

61 "Operation Christmas Child Shoeboxes," YouTube, November 14, 2017, accessed December 9, 2017, https://www.youtube.com/watch?v=ReO-muTWr5E, 0:46. Of note, this represents an excellent example of a conscious attempt by this family to form their own children into a particular Christian narrative.

62 "Operation Christmas Child Shoeboxes," 8:17.

Both of the meanings Jessica ascribes to her family's shoebox associated practices represent enactments of her own aesthetic commitments. The first of the two, the commitment that the box represents an interchangeable unit of divine love that enables children in other countries to know about Jesus, enacts OCC's aesthetic commitments as they relate to materiality. Ironically, Christmas is the time of year Christians specifically celebrate divine materiality. In the words of the apostle John, "The Word became flesh and made his dwelling among us."[63] The immaterial become material—physically present. The incarnation represents an event that instantiates an overabundance of meaning. The intent of the sending of shoeboxes from the United States and other countries to children around the world is to connect these children to the meaning of this event. The meaning constructed and the aesthetic commitments enacted by Jessica and her family as they purchase products and pack and ship shoe boxes are not atypical among those who participate in OCC. They represent Jessica and her family's endeavors to make meaning of the event of God becoming flesh, the event of divine materiality. More broadly, they are paradigmatic of similar endeavors broadly among OCC participants, including among its leaders and organizers. This connection can also be observed in our second example of meaning making.

The second example of meaning making and narrative performance comes from a video by Ryan Hemlock in southeastern Pennsylvania. In the video he describes the mechanics of filling shoeboxes for the benefit of "a child in a third world country." He goes on to further that narrative: "A lot of these kids probably fight really hard just to maintain their food and their water every day of their lives, and they don't have time to think about a Christmas present . . . and most importantly, through theses boxes, through these gifts to these kids, we're able to spread the love of Jesus a little bit more. And that's the purpose and the mission behind these boxes."[64] The

63 John 1:14a (NIV).

64 "Operation Christmas Child," YouTube, accessed December 9, 2017, https://www.youtube.com/watch?v=gomtx_28XF8, 0:55.

video then goes on to show a packing party at Gateway Church. In it several tables are set up as stations for the different type of products that go into the shoeboxes, interviewing several packers along the way. Toward the end of the video, as is typical for YouTube vloggers, he asks for subscriptions so that the viewers can see more "vlogging goodness and business updates," and then also frames OCC as "goodness" as well.[65]

As a vlogger Hemlock is performing for his viewers. He obviously endorses the mission of OCC, ultimately concurring that it represents goodness, and thus believes that his participation in the packing of boxes and filming others packing shoeboxes in his church is enacting that goodness and is subsequently a performance of the good life. Interestingly, his enactment of the good life and his projection of it into the lives of others through his vlog represents a social enactment of his aesthetic commitments. He has been shaped by the narrative that the recipients of the shoeboxes are those in third world countries who do not generally receive Christmas presents. As such he is describing an imagination shaped by OCC's aesthetic commitments and his actions represent a remedy created for a challenge that has been framed in largely spiritual terms. His actions then embody a dramatic performance of a narrative that intends to project good into the lives of those who receive shoeboxes.

In addition, these aesthetic commitments have shaped a particular notion of the good that is embodied by Ryan and itself instantiates these aesthetic commitments.[66] More important than his words is

---

65 "Operation Christmas Child," 4:08.

66 This of course would make sense if there exists a relatively proportional relationship between the notions of the good, the true, and the beautiful as argued for example by von Balthasar (see *Theo-Drama*, vol. 1, *Prolegomena*). The good could then be framed as a social performance of an individual or community's aesthetic commitments, or that which they consider beautiful. However, Hemlock employs the notion of the good with a certain liberality that subverts its significance. Of course Hemlock is not making a philosophical or theological statement about "the good" and as such the rigor of this analysis may seem heavy handed. My intent is not to provide a rigorous examination of his words, but of the relationship between his actions and his words.

the narrative thread in Hemlock's video as it is visually framed and enacted by him and those he films. The good can be framed as both that which benefits Hemlock and that which he perceives might benefit others from afar.

Both of these axes provide insight into the aesthetic processes that form the practices of OCC participants. This notion of the good life is being dramatically performed for others and is thus aesthetically perceived by those witnessing other's performances of the good life. Framed in this manner, each of the YouTube videos represent edited and packaged enactments of a good life imagined by each of the videos' creators with the intention of projecting the meaning of that good life into the experiences of those who watch their videos. This narrative projection is occurring regardless of whether the calculus of this projection is articulated by the creators of these videos. In addition, the practices of OCC participants are dramatic performances of the aesthetic commitments fostered and cultivated through OCC's aesthetic texts and material culture. They help one understand the vision of the good life that forms each participant's affections, imaginations, and practices.

OCC AND EVANGELICAL AESTHETICS

These aesthetic texts and the aesthetic commitments they instantiate then also offer insights into Evangelical formation and identity. Writers often frame Evangelicalism in terms of its conservative politics, anti-institutional dispositions, the privileging of traditional gender roles, sentimentality, and vernacular theology. In the aesthetic texts and practices of OCC one can see Evangelicalism in terms of its aesthetic—for example, the manner in which its theological and aesthetic commitments to creation and materiality effect the aesthetic texts Evangelicalism produces, the practices those commitments animate, and the affections and dispositions of participants.

CHAPTER 6

K-Love and Aesthetic Formation

> K-Love is not just a radio network. K-Love is like an outlet in your wall. Only instead of powering your living room lamp, it empowers you with the love, hope, and peace found only in Jesus Christ. You hear it in the music, you feel it in the prayers of our staff and pastors.
>
> —K-Love,
> "What Happens When You Support K-Love?"

Every day millions of Evangelicals across the United States listen to the nationwide chain of radio stations known as K-Love. In their cars on the way to soccer practice, in their homes as they eat breakfast, and in their earbuds as they work out, they are all listening to the same songs, banter, and prayers. The radio stations have become a valued part of their everyday routine, a firm marker of their Evangelical identity, and an affectionately anticipated personal and devotional pleasure. According to the Educational Media Foundation (EMF), the nonprofit organization that owns and operates K-Love and its sister station Air 1, these two radio networks engage around 20 million listeners every week.[1] The foundation reaches these listeners by employing more than one thousand radio stations and radio

1 Jim Harrington, "Nor-Cal Born K-Love Celebrates 40 Years of Music and Ministry," *The Mercury News*, April 18, 2022, accessed April 24, 2024, https://

repeaters. They maintain a broadcast presence in all fifty states.[2] For many Evangelical Christians, K-Love represents an integral part of their being an Evangelical in the world.

K-Love is also a fundamental part of its audience's ongoing formation as Evangelicals, through the listeners' affections, imaginations, and practices. Just as the aesthetics of OCC have played a part in the formation of Evangelicalism over the past decades, so K-Love has played a pivotal role in underwriting a portion of the Evangelical aesthetic and contributing to their subsequent moral formation.

K-LOVE AND CONTEMPORARY CHRISTIAN MUSIC

The radio station that would become the K-Love radio network first went on the air on October 15, 1982 as KCLB in Santa Rosa, California. The founder, Bob Fogal, who goes by Bob Anthony on the air, worked as a DJ at several radio stations starting in Los Angeles in 1970. During his tenure at pop and rock radio station KRFC in San Francisco in 1978, the relatively recently converted Christian began to consider what a Christian KRFC might sound like.[3] On a yellow legal pad he envisioned a "positive alternative" to stations like KRFC, but one devoid of "Christian-ese." Fogal notes of the first K-Love station, "The jocks were encouraged to talk about God, the Bible and spiritual principles, but speak in ordinary everyday language. No churchy lingo."[4] In his conceptualization of K-Love Fogal envisioned on-air talent who would speak in everyday language free of theological or ecclesiological language that might represent

---

www.mercurynews.com/2022/04/17/norcal-born-k-love-radio-celebrates-40-years-of-music-and-ministry/.

2 "Educational Media Foundation," Educational Media Foundation, accessed April 25, 2024, https://www.emfmedia.com/.

3 Ted Semper, "Bob Anthony Fogal Interview," HisAir.net, October 16, 2022, accessed April 25, 2024, https://www.hisair.net/bob-anthony-fogal-interview/.

4 Semper, "Bob Anthony Fogal Interview."

a high bar of entry for the listener. Fogal was not alone however in growing K-Love into what it is today. Key to its growth and expansion was eventual general manager and head of EMF, Dick Jenkins, who coined K-Love's ubiquitous on-air slogan "Positive and Encouraging" in 1986.[5] EMF was founded at the same time as K-Love, and it owns and governs K-Love's and Air 1's stations, signals, and ministries. Jenkins was also key to K-Love's expansion from one station to the hundreds of stations that now make up its radio network.

K-Love's approach to Christian radio represented something of an innovation at the time, as most radio stations that broadcast Christian content chose to broadcast sermons and messages intended to directly proselytize and teach their listeners. Instead Fogal decided to play music from the nascent genre that would come to be known as contemporary Christian music (CCM). At the time of Fogal's initial imaginings in 1978, the early expressions of CCM had only existed for less than a decade. Growing largely out of the Jesus People movement that had sprung up in Southern California in the late 1960s, artists such as Larry Norman, Andraé Crouch, Mylon Lefevre, Agape, Love Song, 2nd Chapter of Acts, Daniel Amos, Randy Stonehill, and Keith Green and Melody Green represented the first draft of the collective project of translating their personal faiths in Jesus into the language of pop and rock music. As the industry grew, it would come to embody and instantiate what Fogal would frame as his five *E*'s, which would govern K-Love's vision of ministry: Evangelize, Educate, Edify, Exhort, and Encourage.[6] Fogal would go on to use their music, and the music of many others, to try to accomplish these ends. He recognized music's power to shape the listener's affections and imagination.

Just as CCM grew out of the Jesus People movement in Southern California, the Jesus People movement had grown out of the

5 Katie Thornton, "Jesus Take the Dial," *Rolling Stone*, February 2024.

6 Semper, "Bob Anthony Fogal Interview"; see also Leah Payne, *God Gave Rock & Roll to You: A History of Contemporary Christian Music* (Oxford University Press, 2023), 40, 41.

Pentecostal/Charismatic renewal movement that swept through not only Holiness and Pentecostal churches in the 1960s but had found its way into mainline and Catholic churches as well.[7] The Jesus People movement began in earnest after the Summer of Love in 1967 and included those who had at one time identified as hippies, but had become disillusioned with the movement, finding that their experience was not consistent with their expectations or ideals.[8] As many turned to Christianity, they found that the Christian communities most willing to receive and accept them were Pentecostal and Charismatic communities.[9] In addition, the radically spiritual and even mystical experiences endemic to Charismatic expressions of Christianity seemed most like home to many of these new converts. For many, the spiritually ecstatic experiences common in Pentecostalism represented a familiar echo to the spiritual experiences and histories they had brought into these communities.[10]

As the Jesus People movement and this new group of Christians grew, they brought their love for rock music with them into the church. Interestingly, while the notion of bringing rock music into the church in the late 1960s may seem novel, as Evangelicals broadly condemned the music, believing it promoted alcohol use and sexual promiscuity, it was not novel to Holiness and Pentecostal churches generally. This is because rock and roll's sound was at least partially rooted in both African American church music and the music of

7 James K. A. Smith, *Thinking in Tongues: Pentecostal Contributions to Christian Philosophy* (Eerdmans, 2010), v. Pentecostalism itself is generally considered to have come into existence as a result of the Azusa Street revivals (1906–1913) in Los Angeles, though that understanding is not uncontested, as some Pentecostal scholars point to a similar revival in Topeka, Kansas. It however was itself rooted in Methodism and the Wesleyan-Holiness movement that had sprung out of Methodism in the late nineteenth century alongside expressions of African and African American Christian spirituality.

8 Payne notes, "Rather than drug-fueled spiritual insight, free love, peaceful protests, a rejection of materialism, and a rock-and-roll renaissance, they found spiritual emptiness, excess, addiction, sexually transmitted diseases, homelessness, and exploitation" (40).

9 Payne, *God Gave Rock & Roll to You*, 40.

10 Payne, *God Gave Rock & Roll to You*, 40.

white and black Holiness and Pentecostal churches in the southern United States.[11] So while new to the Pentecostal and Charismatic churches in Southern California, these songwriters and musicians shared the aesthetic DNA of their southern cousins alongside their disposition for affect-forward, ecstatic experiences, even as part of their liturgies. In addition, because those writing and creating this rock music inspired by their Christian faith came to the music out of the Charismatic and Pentecostal tradition, the music of CCM also commonly shared many of Pentecostalism's dispositional and doctrinal commitments, including an apocalyptic premillennial dispensationalism, and an emphasis on an authentic, affective, expressive faith.[12]

As CCM developed through the 1980s and 1990s it came to depend on Christian bookstores such as Lifeway and Family Christian Stores to both sell and curate their products. Their largest and most significant commercial demographic were suburban white mothers who would buy the music for both themselves and their children, employing the music as a type of aesthetic catechesis.[13] As such, CCM became a formational tool for Evangelical mothers endeavoring to raise their children in their faith.[14] However, the rise of online stores such as Amazon and the advent of sharable mp3s and streaming in the 2000s led to the commercial decline of Christian bookstores and with it their status as both curator and gatekeeper for CCM. With no institutional gatekeeper, CCM's audience found it more difficult to determine which artists were acceptably Christian

11 Payne, *God Gave Rock & Roll to You*, 26.

12 Payne, *God Gave Rock & Roll to You*, 43, 47. Payne notes that an example of CCM's commitment to a premillennial dispensationalism can be seen in Larry Norman's song "I Wish We'd All Been Ready."

13 Here it is important to remember that while CCM as a project does represent a type of aesthetic religious instruction, it is a multibillion dollar business while simultaneously representing a part of the listener's personal devotional activity. As such, CCM represents a particularly complex set of personal and corporate practices alongside a set of individual engagements and dispositions. See Payne, *God Gave Rock & Roll to You*, 4.

14 Payne, *God Gave Rock & Roll to You*, 52, 58.

and which were not. Artists such as Switchfoot, Dashboard Confessional, Creed, The Fray, Lifehouse, P.O.D., Sixpence None the Richer, and Jars of Clay made these distinctions even more difficult with their successes in the larger mainstream markets, as all of these artists made use of Christian imagery or had connections to the Christian music industry.[15] This ambiguity, along with the growth of pop and rock music employed liturgically in churches as a means of expressing worship, led to worship music essentially supplanting CCM as the primary musical expression of Evangelical popular culture. In short, it seems it was far easier to discern worship music's bona fides than it was to determine whether the music from a band like Creed represented a true articulation of an authentic faith in Jesus. Interestingly, this development only increased Pentecostalism's influence within Evangelicalism.

The rise of the use of pop and rock music to express worship in church settings was a development that ran parallel to the onset and the growth of CCM. The liturgical inclusion of pop and rock music started in the 1970s and 1980s with writers such as Keith Green and Melody Green, Rich Mullins, and Michael W. Smith; however, the trend toward contemporary worship music (CWM) accelerated considerably in the 1990s with the rise of recordings from churches and organizations such as Vineyard, Maranatha!, and Integrity, which was music that had been written for liturgical purposes that were intended to serve largely Pentecostal and Charismatic congregations.[16] While this music did not find a wide hearing within non-Charismatic Evangelical congregations, such as Southern Baptist or Presbyterian communities, there were songs that did find their way into these worship services. Many popular songs that were used in Evangelical liturgical settings, such as "Lord I Lift Your Name on High," "Every Move I Make," and "Shout to the Lord" originated in these Pentecostal or Charismatic settings. The latter of the three originated with Hillsong Church, which would continue to grow

15 Payne, *God Gave Rock & Roll to You*, 130–31, 158–61.
16 Payne, *God Gave Rock & Roll to You*, 124.

through the years between 2000 and 2010 as a significant source of both Charismatic and Evangelical worship music.

As the 1990s gave way to the 2000s the use of worship music originating in Pentecostal and Charismatic congregations would continue to grow in Evangelical churches. Alongside the use of these songs, many churches would also begin to employ Pentecostal liturgy templates, in particular beginning their services with sets of songs as opposed to singing single hymns. Christian worship scholars Swee Hung Lim and Lester Ruth note that this centrality of music in contemporary Christian worship is rooted in Pentecostal liturgical and devotional dispositions.[17] Payne suggests that the Evangelical embrace of CCM and subsequently CWM has played a significant role in the Pentecostalization of Evangelicalism, particularly of white Evangelicalism in the United States.[18]

Evangelicalism has not become Pentecostal or Charismatic, though Pentecostalism falls under the larger umbrella of Evangelicalism. Pentecostal denominations such as the Assemblies of God have been members of the National Association of Evangelical's coalition since its founding. However, over the past forty years Evangelicalism has come to embody many of the aesthetic commitments and practices unique to its Pentecostal cousins. This is an important and noteworthy development in Evangelicalism that profoundly effects how we conceive of the aesthetic processes forming Evangelicals. More importantly, this Pentecostalization of Evangelicalism also affects how one understands the aesthetics of K-Love, as K-Love has played a part in embedding both CCM and CWM into the loves, affections, and practices of Evangelicals across the United States. In doing so, K-Love has participated in embedding a particularly Pentecostal or Charismatic way of seeing, perceiving, and being into Evangelical aesthetics and practices.

---

17 Swee Hung Lim and Lester Ruth, *Lovin' on Jesus: A Concise History of Contemporary Worship* (Abingdon Press, 2017), 98.

18 Payne, *God Gave Rock & Roll to You*, 194.

PENTECOSTAL AESTHETICS AND K-LOVE

Pentecostalism does not imply the presence of a unique set of doctrines, or a set of propositional ideas; instead, according to James K. A. Smith, Pentecostalism represents "an affective constellation of practices and embodied 'rituals.'"[19] Pentecostalism also embodies a particularly affective manner of understanding the world.[20] To use the philosopher Charles Taylor's terminology, it embodies a particular social imaginary: the "tacit, affective understanding of the world that constitutes the 'background' of our being and doing."[21] As such Pentecostalism denotes a particular style or manner of embodiment alongside a particular set of dispositions toward both the social and material world. Smith goes on to name five embodied dispositions that fund Pentecostal and Charismatic practices and identity: "1) A position of radical openness to God, and in particular, an openness to God doing something differently or new. 2) An 'enchanted' theology of creation and culture that perceives the material creation as 'charged' with the presence of the Spirit 3) A non-dualistic affirmation of embodiment and material expressed in an emphasis on physical healing 4) Because of the emphasis on experience, a theology rooted in an affective, narrative epistemology 5) An eschatological orientation to mission and justice."[22] The result is a particularly Pentecostal/Charismatic aesthetic. This connection between Pentecostal dispositions and Pentecostal aesthetics and aesthetic formation can be traced through various Pentecostal practices.

Of particular interest, as it relates to the aesthetic formation framework that has been argued for thus far, is the importance of

19 Smith, *Thinking in Tongues*, ix.

20 Smith, *Thinking in Tongues*, 26.

21 Smith, *Thinking in Tongues*, 29.

22 Smith, *Thinking in Tongues*, 11, 12. Smith's list of course is neither exhaustive nor exclusive. Christians from other traditions, be they Protestant, Catholic, or Orthodox, would likely identify with one or several of these dispositions. However, what is named here does offer a succinct taxonomy of an identifiable set of markers to help account for that which distinguishes Pentecostal Christians from their non-Pentecostal, non-Charismatic counterparts.

affect and narrative to the formation of Pentecostal dispositions and identities. To that end, Smith notes the formational power of testimonies (the practice of congregants speaking publicly before the congregation of their experiences of how they perceive God to have been working in their lives, typically for their good) within Pentecostal liturgies. He argues that in light of Pentecostal practices and the emphasis on experience, story precedes propositions and imagination precedes intellection for Pentecostal dispositions.[23] Not only does this set of dispositions allow for the Pentecostal Christian to write their experiences and the circumstances that constitute their lives into God's story or redemption, it also creates the space for a type of affective, experiential knowledge that cannot be reduced to a proposition.[24] Here recall novelist Flannery O'Connor's assertion that "a story is a way to say something that can't be said any other way, and it takes every word in the story to say what the meaning is. You tell a story because a statement would be inadequate."[25] Through the practice of offering testimonies, affective processes of formation are active as congregants share their stories of how they perceive God working in their lives, providing a narrative shape to their own lives while simultaneously affectively directing the imaginations of those listening toward a particular set of narratively articulated meanings embedded in their stories.[26]

---

23 Smith, *Thinking in Tongues*, 43.

24 Smith, *Thinking in Tongues*, 50, 61, 63. Smith cites an oft-repeated truism within Pentecostal communities: "I know that I know that I know" as an idiomatic articulation of this type of affective knowledge (26).

25 O'Connor, *Mystery and Manners*, 96.

26 This embodied approach to meaning making does not stand alone within Pentecostal approaches to liturgy and worship, and that is the point. Pentecostalism is imbued in congregants through fundamentally embodied, aesthetic processes. Lim and Ruth note some of the ways in which these dispositions and this aesthetic manifest themselves, both in Pentecostal/Charismatic and traditionally Evangelical congregations. They note that the mainstreaming of physical expressiveness in Evangelical worship (for example the raising of hands or raising of one's eyes during worship through music) has its roots in Pentecostal embodiment, as does the notion that outward expressions of worship should represent authentic embodiments of inner dispositions. (See

Pentecostal spirituality and Pentecostal aesthetics are relevant to the role K-Love plays in the aesthetic moral formation of Evangelicals. Its relevance lies in the Pentecostal and Charismatic roots of CCM and CWM. If both CCM and CWM are rooted, even partially, in Pentecostal spirituality and aesthetics then those aesthetic dispositions and commitments are contributing to the formation of the affections and imaginations of the Evangelicals that love these songs and artists.[27]

THE AESTHETICS OF K-LOVE

K-love's aesthetic is instantiated first and foremost in its primary texts: the songs it chooses to broadcast. However, its aesthetic goes beyond its songs as K-Love's DJs and its produced commercials and

Lim and Ruth, *Lovin' on Jesus,* 24). One can place the expectation of divine encounter in the midst of congregational worship through music alongside these Pentecostally inflected liturgical expectations, dispositions, and practices. These represent just a few examples of the way in which Pentecostal and Pentecostally influenced Evangelicals engage their bodies as a means of expressing inward experiences, and how those bodily practices and dispositions come to affect their imaginations and affections. Lim and Ruth also argue that the adoption of Pentecostal approaches to worship and liturgy have led to changes in the perception of time, both in the short term and in the long terms (in both liturgical rhythms and the liturgical calendar), even eroding the notion of Sunday as a day set aside for gathering as a community of faith (31–39). It has also led to changes in the liturgical space, amending the notion of what represents the liturgical centers within the worship space (moving from liturgical centers like the altar, the pulpit, the baptismal, and the presider's chair to liturgical centers like the platform, the sound booth, the lighting board, and the videographer's space; 45–50). They also argue that the Pentecostal approach to worship results in a particular set of foci in the music. The lyrics commonly focus on the direct relationship between God and the singer, often involving prayers for divine presence. Subjects that are rarely included, or that are outright absent, include intercession for others, confession of sin or fault, or expressions of lament or distress (99–101).

27 Payne notes that the contemporary popularity of worship music from the likes of Hillsong and Bethel within Evangelical circles demonstrates that Pentecostal and Charismatic Christians were the winners of the worship wars (151).

testimonies also contribute to its aesthetic and the subsequent formation that occurs among its listeners, as do the videos that they produce and post online. K-love's playlists of songs date back more than forty years. This breadth of music represents a set of songs far too extensive for the project at hand.[28] As such, we will place our focus on K-Love's list of its own top fifteen songs from both 2022 and 2023. These represent the most played songs on K-Love over that two-year span.[29] Interestingly, this set of thirty songs finds a strong musical and aesthetic resonance with the content and contours of a Pentecostally influenced church service.

Of K-Love's top thirty songs for 2022 and 2023, eleven can be classified as worship songs fit for use within a liturgical setting. As examples, as of late April 2024 Brandon Heath's "Gratitude" was the fourth-most used song in worship services, as recorded by Christian Copyright Licensing International (CCLI).[30] Phil Wickham's "This Is Our God" was the twenty-second–most used song nationally. Matt Maher's "The Lord's Prayer" was the seventy-eighth most used and We the Kingdom's "Jesus Does" was the 221st-most used song. Each of these represent parts of K-Love's top fifteen most played lists for 2022 and 2023. Alongside these worship songs, fifteen of the thirty most

---

28 K-Love plays into the nostalgia for previous eras of CCM by broadcasting "K-Love 2000s" and "K-Love 90s" as separate HD stations available as adjacent to its primary broadcast. They are also available to stream online.

29 For a complete list of these songs see Lindsay Williams, "The Top 30 Songs of 2023," K-Love, December 28, 2023, https://www.klove.com/music/blog/musicnews/the-top-30-songs-of-2023-7025, and Williams, "The Top 30 Songs of 2022," K-Love, January 1, 2023, https://www.klove.com/music/blog/music/k-loves-top-30-songs-of-2022-4473.

30 CCLI is a private company that allows a licensee, such as a church, to use copyrighted music for worship purposes without the use of that song representing an infringement of that copyright. It also tracks songs used through online programs and apps such as Planning Center Online, which churches use to plan worship services, store music and arrangements for musicians, and organize and plan practices for those musicians. Because of this they can record the frequency of song uses across churches. Their list represents something like the top forty of worship music. See "What We Provide," CCLI, accessed April 29, 2024, https://us.ccli.com/what-we-provide/.

popular songs on K-Love can be classified as musical testimonies. As such, they musically mirror the role of the stories told in church of the ways in which the singer has experienced Gods' good work in their lives. The remaining four of K-Love's top songs from 2022 and 2023 can be classified as either encouragement, invitation, or prayer. However, each represents essentially a play on the testimonial format, amending the "I" pronoun key to the testimonial format into the pronoun "you," almost encouraging the listener toward their own type of testimony that mirrors the singer's encouragement and the testimonial format.[31]

With K-Love's musical focus on worship and testimony, it creates a continuous, interlaced loop of the two most aesthetically significant portions of a Pentecostally influenced worship service. Throw in its prerecorded scriptural lessons, minisermons if you will, and you have each of the primary beats of a church service repeated continuously throughout the day. In doing so, it has created something like a continuously broadcast liturgy loop that allows the listener to enter and leave as they chose. The fundamentally aesthetic nature of each portion of this content greatly contributes to the formation of the listener's affections, dispositions, and practices, as does the nature of liturgy. This is simply what is accomplished through these aesthetic forms. The question then arises as to what end K-Loves listeners are being formed toward, alongside the question of K-Love's envisioned formational telos.

Those formational ends can be seen in the manner in which the lyrics are instantiated in the musical form of the songs that K-love curates for broadcast. While popular artists such as TobyMac, Jeremy Camp, and David Crowder may have an advantage in gaining airplay, for a station like K-Love, the content of the song precedes the artist in

31 These categorizations do not represent discreet, iron-clad taxonomies. Within this set of songs there are testimony songs that include elements of worship and worship songs that include elements of testimony. These are intended as broad categorizations attempting to articulate the narrative directions of the songs for the purposes of articulating the role they play in the formation of affections and dispositions.

terms of airplay criteria. In this context, content is king. Payne argues that the history and development of CCM can provide key insights into the development of Evangelicalism, noting the CCM music sales charts "displayed what sorts of ideas about God, the world, and the people of God were bankable evangelical theologies."[32] Bankable also means that the musical articulations of CCM represented something like the pop culture articulations of Evangelical theology and ideals. In essence the marriage of the musical form and the lyric represented affective, narrative articulations of what the consuming Evangelical public believes about how both Christianity and the world ought to be, and therefore represents an articulation of the formational ends they ought to be aiming for. With that in mind it seems fitting to turn to several of the popular worship songs from 2022 and 2023 that were broadcast on K-Love, followed by several of the most popular testimonial songs from the same time period.

K-Love and Worship Music

The starting point will be the four most popular worship songs, listed previously from Brandon Heath, Phil Wickham, Matt Maher and We the Kingdom. The songs show a good bit of variety in terms of their content. Brandon Heath's "Gratitude" is an expression of both gratitude and worship directed toward the "king" and the "Lord." Phil Wickham's "This Is Our God" bleeds over into testimony asking the listener to recall the prison of sin and shame Jesus had released them from, along with the giants of death and the grave that are now themselves dead, and the fear that Jesus's faithfulness has overcome.

32 Payne, *God Gave Rock & Roll to You*, 5. Interestingly, she also notes, "Sometimes these off-the-books ideas aligned with official denominational or congregational teaching; sometimes they did not. Through the market, consumers challenged—and in some cases overturned—the traditional, institutional authority of their pastors, congregations, or denominations" (5). This speaks to not only the Pentecostalization of Evangelicalism, but to the notion that capitalism and the capitalist notion of the market have played a potentially fundamental part in that process.

He goes on to sing that Jesus accomplished these acts for humanity because love, grace, and salvation are simply who God is. Matt Maher's "The Lord's Prayer (It's Yours)" is almost simply the Lord's Prayer set to anthemic arena pop. We the Kingdom's "Jesus Does" recalls Jesus's lordship over creation, concern for the orphan and the widow, and forgiveness of sinners, offering praise as a response to these and other divine acts.

Each of these songs represent orthodox articulations of Evangelical theological commitments, though there are several Pentecostal-influenced inflections and metaphors that find their way into these songs. Brandon Heath's chorus notes that he throws up his hands to praise God. Phil Wickham employs the popular Pentecostal metaphor of facing one's giants, naming death and the grave as two of them. Neither Maher nor We the Kingdom include any theological commitments in their songs that would not likely be embraced across Evangelicalism. In terms of content, while all pointing toward worship of similar conceptions of the trinitarian God, they all accomplish those ends in different ways, articulating different portions of those commitments. They do, however, all share something in common in their form, a sense that the emotive embodiment of the content being sung represents a fundamentally good and fundamentally Christian use of the body and the emotions.

The power of the formational aesthetic comes into focus as one affectively feels the ways in which the bodies and voices of the artists are being used to embody their commitments to worship. Returning to Heath's "Gratitude," after the song's bridge and the self-admonishment to unleash the lion in his lungs, Heath does just that in the ensuing interlude. As strings swell, Heath voices what might best be described as a well-controlled wail as he sings the words "praise the Lord." Heath's wail represents an authentic embodiment of his own feelings and commitments while simultaneously representing an invitation for the listener to employ their own bodies to similar ends. It represents a musical invitation for bodies and affections to share in this emotive expression of praise and worship. Heath is not alone in this regard. Each performance of the songs noted above instantiate a similar sense of emotive, embodied worship, though perhaps not quite as intensely as Heath does. Though not a part of the broadcast of these songs on K-Love, this emotive embodiment can be seen in the music videos produced for each of these songs. Heath in his video for "Gratitude" sways with the music in the bridge and the interlude, forcefully waving his arms, alternating between looking toward the sky and doubling over as he sings, raising his hands often in the process. Wickham bounces and dances with the midtempo music in his video, also forcefully waving his hands, often to the beat, as a type of emphasis on what is being sung. Maher is not quite as expressive with his body as Heath and Wickham are; however, Maher's video includes an audience, absent from the other two videos. Here the audience represents the expressions of this emotive embodiment, actively expressing the affective experience of worship with their bodies as they sing the words of the Lord's Prayer. Maher's song also offers a nod to the emotive aesthetic often associated with musical expressions of worship in the African American church, beginning the song with the sounds of bluesy seventh chords on a Hammond organ and growing into the call and answer of a gospel choir. We the Kingdom also borrows from a type of nostalgia, writing a country-inflected worship song. The video ends with the entire band jumping to beat of the song, often with the heads thrown back and the arms raised while they sing in a rather ecstatic community expression of worship.[33]

So while each of these songs represent largely orthodox poetic articulations and therefore a type of catechetical reinforcement of propositionally articulated Christian theological commitments, they achieve their formational effects both through the embodiment necessary for the creation of music, and through this Pentecostally inflected style of emotive embodiment native to Pentecostally

33 In addition, several of the band members sport wet hair and clothes having emerged from a river in the video, offering an image likely intended to evoke baptism.

inflected worship practices.[34] This approach has become fundamental to both the formation of Evangelical affections and dispositions, and to the formation of Evangelical identity. These songs and their accompanying videos represent embodied articulations of what their creators and broadcasters understand as the appropriate uses of the body as a means to express one's affections, commitments, and dispositions. In each of these, and other cases instantiated in the worship music broadcast by K-Love, these uses of the body are fundamentally emotive, even ecstatic. The songs broadcast on K-Love that represent musical testimonies, however, follow a slightly different road toward the formation of the listener's affections and imagination.

K-Love and the Music of Testimony

Testimonies fundamentally represent both an individual and community meaning-making project. The songs that K-Love broadcasts that take the form of testimonies accomplish something very similar, through similarly narratively embodied means, but adding the embodied layer of music on top (or perhaps underneath) the storytelling alone. The testimony songs broadcast by K-Love generally begin with the naming a circumstance or practice that the storyteller is struggling with presently, or a part of the circumstances, practices, or relationships that characterized the storyteller's life before their conversion to Christianity. Following a similar template, this dark start is common in the testimony songs broadcast on K-Love. Singer Micah Taylor acknowledges his experience of shame, regret, and failure in his up-tempo, almost danceable song "I See Grace." Jeremy Camp begins his anthemic pop song "Anxious Heart" singing of the paralyzing embodied experience of anxiety and the weakness that

34 In the liner notes to *Accelerando*, Jazz pianist Vijay Iyer notes of the embodied process of music making, "Music is action: the sound of bodies in motion. When we hear a rhythm, we imagine the act that gave rise to it. Some call it neural mirroring, or empathy. Music and dance are linked in this way: bodies listening to bodies" (The Vijay Iyer Trio, *Accelerando*, ACT Records, 2012).

he experienced as part of it. Rachel Lampa acknowledges the anxiety that often accompanies success and the associated fear of failure in her ballad "Somebody to You."[35] In these songs, however, the darkness does not stay long. What follows the description of the darkness is a description of the ways the storyteller or singer has experienced God overcoming that darkness for and in them.

Micah Tyler describes the ways in which his experience of God's grace in the person of Jesus has wiped away his experiences of shame, regret, and failure, drawing on the scriptural narrative parables of the prodigal son and the ninety-nine sheep, both from Luke 15. Jeremy Camp sings that God represents the light in his dark and the calm for his anxious heart. Rachel Lampa reminds herself that she is somebody in Jesus with nothing to prove to others, and therefore should not fear their judgments or negativity. And while each may go on to acknowledge other difficulties in their own ways, they each instantiate the common notion that their reliance on God is fundamental to overcoming their dark experiences (as it generally does in the testimonies offered in liturgical settings).[36] This com-

---

35 Of note, Rachel Lampa is one of only five solo female singers, and her song one of only six, in the set of the top fifteen songs from 2022 and 2023 (though a female vocalist is a member of the band We the Kingdom). Of those six songs, only three are sung entirely solo by the female singer. The other three are sung as duets with male counterparts. The relatively few female artists included in K-Love's playlist does raise the question as to the reasons why.

36 Of note, many of the Psalms employ a similar format; however, many do not. It seems there would be little room in these musical testimonial narratives, and little room on K-Love, for expressions similar for example to Ps 88, which does not end with a clear account of the psalmist's experience of their reliance on God. In Ps 88, the Psalmist shares their dark experiences, writing, "You have put me in the lowest pit, in the darkest depths. Your wrath lies heavily on me; you have overwhelmed me with all your waves. You have taken from me my closest friends and have made me repulsive to them. I am confined and cannot escape; my eyes are dim with grief" (Ps 88:6–9 NIV). The psalmist continues, "But I cry to you for help, LORD; in the morning my prayer comes before you. Why, LORD, do you reject me and hide your face from me?" (vv. 13–14) and finishes this expression of this experience of darkness writing, "Your wrath has swept over me; your terrors have destroyed me. All day long they surround me like a flood; they have completely engulfed me. You have taken from me friend

mon, even expected, and fundamentally comforting narrative story arc represents a set of aesthetic texts that shape the affections and dispositions of its listeners to love these types of stories. This use of this narrative arc is not confined to the songs on K-Love. It is also reinforced by recorded testimonies that share the same narrative arc and by stories shared by the DJs, both the stories shared with them by listeners and their own stories. K-Love further reinforces this testimonial narrative arc in interviews and produced narrative videos on their website and on their YouTube channel.

The repeated use the narrative story arc that begins with dark and painful experiences that are overcome and replaced with love, grace, and even joy becomes the expectation or expected template for the normative Evangelical experience. The repeated broadcast of these musical narratives, alongside the emotively embodied songs of worship, offer aesthetic expressions of the Evangelical good life, instantiating a particular set of roles for the body and the affections for the Evangelicals that listen. The practices that accompany K-Love's songs of worship and songs of testimony represent the dramatic enaction of the affections and dispositions that are formed through the listener's interactions with these aesthetic texts.

THE PRACTICES OF K-LOVE

K-Love's playlists strongly resemble the beats of a Pentecostal worship service, in particular the emotively embodied music and the practice

---

and neighbor—darkness is my closest friend" (vv. 16–18). Here the psalmist names and remains in the experience of darkness without continuing to an account of God overcoming it. This honest and gut-wrenching poetic expression of this writer's experience of loneliness and even something akin to divine abandonment is included in what is often framed as Israel's book of hymns. The absence of narratives like Ps 88 and other psalms of lament (whether psalms of personal lament like this one, or psalms that lament the absence of justice) raises questions as to why musical accounts of these types of narratives are absent from K-Love's playlists.

of testimony. The practices of K-Love's listeners embody the affections, imaginations, and dispositions that have been formed through their interactions with K-Love's songs and other aesthetic texts. To that end, three sets of embodied practices funded by K-Love's aesthetic texts demonstrate the ways in which its listeners have been formed: practices that demonstrate the authenticity of their worship and testimony, most commonly framed by K-Love as acts of kindness and service; the practice of listening itself; and the practice of donating money to K-Love, which itself can be framed as a practice that also demonstrates the authenticity of the listener's worship and testimony.

Practices—Acts of Kindness and Service

One of the devotional commitments articulated over the air on K-Love, whether by listeners, DJs, or the songs, is the commitment to living in a way that is consistent with one's faith, where the actions the listener performs authentically reflects faith in Jesus. This way of life serves as a type of embodied evidence of the individual's testimony. While proselytization or evangelism ranks high in that constellation of actions among K-Love listeners, acts of kindness and service are a common way of evidencing the authenticity of one's faith (aside from giving).[37] Every record of the call to these acts of kindness and service, and any record of listeners' practices as they relate to these calls, all originate with K-Love. As such, they represent a methodological difficulty. Unlike OCC, there is a dearth of online videos of people documenting their practices associated with these types of calls to action.[38] However, K-Love's calls for action still rep-

37 We must note that acts of kindness and service are often enacted for the sole purpose of proselytization, as we saw earlier in Franklin Graham's articulation of why Samaritan's Purse serves the victims of natural disasters and wars.

38 Interestingly, there is a video of an OCC packing party in Sacramento that documents participants' attendance of the party because it was announced on and promoted by K-Love. However, even it was produced by the local K-Love station in Sacramento. See KloveSacramento, "Operation Christmas Child," YouTube, November 16, 2009, accessed May 1, 2024,

resent a call toward a normative expression of an Evangelical faith in Jesus. The expressions offer a glimpse of K-love's understanding of normative discipleship and the Christian good life, and as such represents a particular good telos that K-love believes Evangelicals' actions should be heading toward.

These called for acts of kindness and service often do not require much from the listener. As an example, a video posted on K-Love's YouTube page in November of 2021 encourages listeners to pay for, pray for, and leave a note of encouragement for the person behind them in a drive-through as "a small token of your love, God."[39] This particular set of practices was part of a short-term program encouraging these types of acts titled "Share the Love." In the video a DJ named Lauree (K-Love typically only shares the first names of their DJs) is filmed doing just this, noting that she was blending notes of encouragement, which were an emphasis at K-Love at the time, with action.[40] Two other DJs, Scott and Kelli, encourage listeners to write a note of encouragement to their neighbors sharing what they appreciate about them, noting that "those few words that you write can make all the difference in the world."[41] While this "Share the Love" event from November of 2021 was a short-term project, it is part of an larger ongoing project called "Make a Difference Mondays."[42] These acts represent an effort toward a type of public discipleship, naming and embodying formational ends, setting listeners' affections and imaginations toward those ends, and encouraging those listeners to use their bodies to enact those affections.

---

https://www.youtube.com/watch?v=0xBv1lCkE1k&list=PL7P-kPqHqh_efRpmjGiiikhk16qDH4ShS&index=2.

39 K-Love, "Lauree Visits Local Drive-Thru to Surprise Stranger with Free Meal," YouTube, November 19, 2021, accessed May 1, 2024, https://www.youtube.com/watch?v=r49I36i3r6Q&t=2s, 1:40.

40 K-Love, "Lauree Visits Local Drive-Thru," 0:12.

41 K-Love, "Scott & Kelli Are Sharing the Love with Their Neighbors," YouTube, November 15, 2021, accessed May 1, 2024, https://www.youtube.com/watch?v=ho8DSSCJXzA, 1:02.

42 K-Love, "Scott & Kelli Are Sharing the Love," 1:05.

The most direct example of the formation from general embodied practices among K-Love listeners is rooted in the emotive embodied expressions of worship. However, these projects encouraging acts of service and kindness are intended to form the actions of its listeners and are built alongside the music broadcast by K-Love. This is because the music broadcast by K-Love almost exclusively focuses on the artist's, and thus subsequently the listeners', direct relationship to the Father or Jesus (and at times the Holy Spirit). Of the top fifteen songs from 2022 and 2023 only one includes any allusion to the social, often framed as the horizontal, consequences or their faith. The band Consumed by Fire notes the desire to seek God's will and live God's truth in their song "First Things First." The other twenty-nine of the most popular songs on K-Love in 2022 and 2023 represent either a first-person direct address of the artist/listener toward God, often musing on the nature of that relationship, or a second-person imperative directing the listener's attention toward God.

While these calls toward acts of service and kindness represent a portion of the aesthetic formation that occurs among K-Love listeners because of the visual and narrative means of persuasion, it also represents a formation—related to the listener's relationship to God as articulated in K-Love's songs—that must be encouraged by supplemental means. This is because of the relative absence of this type of catechesis in the songs themselves. This type of formation, intended to move from the interiority of the listener's faith to the physical reality of embodied action that dramatically reveals the authenticity and truth of that faith, is not limited on K-Love to acts of service and kindness.

Practices—Listening

For K-Love to exist it needs people to listen. This may seem obvious, but listening as a practice must be mentioned, even if only briefly. I had earlier noted Payne's recognition that CCM simultaneously represented a business, religious instruction, and a devotional activity.[43]

43 See Payne, *God Gave Rock & Roll to You*, 4.

Listening represents the devotional activity portion of that triple relationship. Those who actively choose to listen offer a wide variety of reasons for doing so. Whatever reason they offer, by listening, the active listener expects to yield a positive effect on their life, faith, and practice.

This positive effect can be as simple as placing the listener in a good mood or the experience of being uplifted by the music and talk.[44] Other listeners speak of encountering God through the music. One listener describes driving home in her car and "crying out" when she heard the song "I Need You Now" by the group Plumb, which precipitated an experience of the peace of God falling on her, "like never before."[45] Many cite K-love as an indispensable resource for navigating difficult times. A listener named Bonnie Adams describes overwhelming struggles with her health and family and shares that she had prayed that God would "just take me home."[46] She describes hearing the song "Even If" from the band MercyMe resonating with the lyrics that speak to God using pain for a greater good, even if one is not healed. She cites the experience of hearing that song in that moment as the reason she was able to keep her hope in God.[47] Another listener identified as Crystal cites K-Love's role in seeing her through bouts with addiction. She notes that when she fell away from God it was music along with a church and a community that loved K-Love that brought her back to God.[48] Finally, another listener

44 K-Love, "K-Love Pledge Drive—Listener Testimonies," YouTube, posted April 12, 2012, accessed April 30, 2024, https://www.youtube.com/watch?v=xRX1yXno1GE, 0:06, 0:30.

45 K-Love, "K-LOVE Listener Story: You Make A Positive Difference," YouTube, May 27, 2014, accessed April 30, 2024, https://www.youtube.com/watch?v=dooofLd3cLM, 0:08.

46 K-Love, "God Gave a Listener Hope through K-Love," YouTube, posted September 30, 2022, accessed 5/2/24, https://www.youtube.com/watch?v=fGJHUgZ-jCw, 0:31.

47 K-Love, "God Gave a Listener Hope," 0:52.

48 K-Love, "K-Love Listener Story with Scott," YouTube, posted February 10, 2020, accessed May 2, 2024, https://www.youtube.com/watch?v=S1eVGS1CATo, 0:24.

identified as Jack notes that when his wife was diagnosed with cancer, "K-Love became my everyday sermon."[49] He shares that the first time he heard Katy Nichole's song "In Jesus Name (God of Possible)" it became his prayer anthem, recognizing that "without those songs picking me up, I could have very easily caved in."[50] He finishes suggesting that the "daily sermon" that represents K-Love to him, which he also associated with Jesus's presence, is what he believes gave him the strength to endure the loss of his wife.[51]

Each story is fundamentally rooted in the embodied practice of listening. Within this set of stories, listening becomes its own type of devotional practice. The songs broadcast by K-Love become both the devotional text and the accompanying prayers, with the listener hearing and singing the songs and their musical narratives in their own voices and incorporating them into their own narrative, interlacing the two into something entirely new, but deeply affecting and meaningful for the listener. Many of the testimonials cite particular songs and particular moments where those songs broke open an experience of divine presence or a deeper understanding of divine truth, goodness, or beauty. In each of these, listening itself represents a practice that dramatically embodies the affections that have previously been formed, whether in church settings, among friends, or by prior engagements with K-Love.

Practices—Giving

The final practice funded by K-Love's aesthetic is giving. This combines all three of the practices that make up CCM, mentioned earlier: business, devotional activity, and religious instruction. As such, giving can prove to be a particularly complex practice or set of practices. Of note, of all the practices funded by K-Love's aesthetics, this is

49 K-Love, "How a K-Love Listener Found Hope through Heartache," YouTube, posted October 13, 2023, accessed May 2, 2024, https://www.youtube.com/watch?v=ZvflEwDmK_4, 0:18.

50 K-Love, "How a K-Love Listener Found Hope," 1:00.

51 K-Love, "How a K-Love Listener Found Hope," 1:05.

the only one that is framed as being done in service of others. The motivation for giving, as framed by K-Love, mirrors something of Adam Smith's notion of the role moral sentiments play in moral formation. Listeners are asked to first remember what K-Love has meant to them, and then imagine the value of others receiving the same benefits. In that process, the calls to give are still deeply rooted in the affections and dispositions that are developed through listener's engagements with K-Love's other aesthetic texts. This too can be observed in many of the videos K-Love has posted requesting listener's give to the ministry.

A listener who identified himself as Jerry Eden said that hearing testimonies of experiences of divine encounter when in despair is important to him, citing the Gospel story of the widow giving her two mites at the temple in Luke 21 as a picture of what he believes is his responsibility to faithfully support a ministry that facilitates that type of encounter.[52] Another advertisement employs a similar approach, playing a testimony from an unnamed listener, recorded over the phone, acknowledging the experience of blessing K-Love has brought to her life. The listener goes on to declare, choking back tears, "It's really nice to be able to turn on your radio and hear music about God and how much he loves you, no matter what you've been through."[53] The video then flashed the words, "This is what happens when you give" in blue letters against a white screen, playing on that same sense of responsibility to share the experience of K-Love as a ministry to and a service to others.[54] In another video thanking listeners for their giving, an employee of K-Love directly addresses the viewer, thanking them for their donations and acknowledging that

52 K-Love, "Why Give to K-Love? 'The Reward Is Knowing People's Lives Changed,'" YouTube, posted October 25, 2017, accessed May 2, 2024, https://www.youtube.com/watch?v=M4yMKjUlTM4, 0:07.

53 K-Love, "K-Love—This Is What Happens When You Give," YouTube, posted April 25, 2016, accessed May 2, 2024, https://www.youtube.com/watch?v=j8IFxh8x9Z8, 0:45.

54 K-Love, "This Is What Happens When You Give," 1:02.

it "means the world," for both K-Love and the world itself.[55] She goes on to say, "You have no idea how many people are out there, driving around in their cars, really needing to hear a message of hope and the message that you're providing is that hope in Jesus Christ that they have access to now."[56] Finally, another video records a listener named Nancy noting that she has continually increased her giving to K-Love over the years because she continues to be more and more inspired by it, noting that she has now included K-Love in her legacy estate giving so that she leaves a spiritual legacy along with her material one, and so that K-Love can continue after she is gone.[57]

The practice of giving is of course necessary for a nonprofit organization such as EMF and K-Love to remain in operation; however, the practice of giving is also framed as a type of embodiment of the affections already formed in listeners through K-Love's aesthetics. To explore the relationship between K-Love's aesthetics and practices, the relationship between K-Love's aesthetics and practices along the dramatic axis of embodiment and performance must also be considered, alongside the axis of meaning making and narrative. These dramatic axes help to demonstrate the ways in which K-Love forms Evangelical affections, dispositions, imaginations, and practices in ways that parallel the aesthetic formation that occurs among the participants of OCC.

THE RELATIONSHIP OF K-LOVE'S AESTHETICS AND ITS PRACTICES

The lines of formation that run from OCC's aesthetic texts through to their practices are specific to the moral formation that grows out

55 K-Love, "Thank You—K-Love Is Fully Funded!," YouTube, posted April 27, 2017, accessed May 2, 2024, https://www.youtube.com/watch?v=n-hNsv6NBdo, 1:29.

56 K-Love, "Thank You," 1:37.

57 K-Love, "How K-Love Inspired a Listener to Leave a Legacy," YouTube, posted December 9, 2023, accessed May 2, 2024, https://www.youtube.com/watch?v=g4R2SPnz80k, 0:43.

of K-Love's aesthetic texts. They embody the same two sets of axes that were used to trace the path of aesthetic formation among the participants in OCC: embodiment and performance and meaning making and narrative.

Embodiment and Performance

The practices of K-Love listeners that grow out of their affections and dispositions and embody their aesthetic commitments are impacted by the layered manner in which K-Love frames listener's bodies. Bodies are framed by the songs of K-Love and by K-Love's on-air talent. The roles bodies and performance play in the processes of aesthetic formation can be seen in of the listener's testimonies and the ways they do and do not articulate the manner in which K-Love's songs and programming shapes their practices.

The worship songs played on K-Love generally encourage and even expect an emotively embodied response from their listeners, instantiating the often Pentecostal and Charismatic aesthetic commitments of the artists who write and record the songs. In this way the body, with its hands raised, its head back, its face tilted toward the sky and its voice singing with abandon, is front and center as it relates to the aesthetic expectations and commitments instantiated in K-Love's worship songs.

Here the body is an instrument employed to express affection for and devotion to God. In this way these songs are intended to enlist the body as a means of outwardly expressing a set of internal dispositions. The authenticity of those internal dispositions, and the way those dispositions frame the listener's perception of and experience of the divine, represents an approximate telos for the songs and DJs on K-Love. These experiences represent one of the core reasons K-Love exists.[58] Interestingly, these practices also represent the role social

---

58 K-love articulates their mission this way: "Create and distribute quality and compelling media that inspires and encourages people to have a meaningful relationship with Jesus Christ." ("Mission, Beliefs & Values," K-Love, accessed

forces and the community play in aesthetic formation. This is because these practices, along with the worshipping community's bodily and dispositional expectations, are learned as much through observation and imitation, a type of social catechesis, as they are through what might be called the lyrical catechesis of the worship and testimonial songs played on K-Love. This is because, ironically, as the body is front and center for the expressions of devotion and worship, the body is generally hidden in the lyrics these songs themselves.

The body of course does make appearances in these songs. Using the set of the top thirty songs from K-Love in 2022 and 2023, the body is described in the songs; however, when it is included, it is often included in a metaphorical manner, and not for descriptions of its physicality or its material presence. For example, Micah Tyler in his song "I See Grace" notes that he has seen Jesus's nail-scarred hands both reach out and wipe away mistakes and regrets. Of course, Evangelicals are committed to the tenet that Jesus's incarnation represented a physical reality in time and space. While his observations of that experience can be rooted in the embodied notion of Christ's incarnation, Tyler, of course, was not a witness to the incarnation. This event then, described by Tyler, does not describe a physical reality, but a metaphorical description of an emotional or internal experience. Tyler is not alone; the notion of Jesus's incarnational embodiment also shows up briefly in other songs. For example, the band For King and Country recognizes Jesus's body that was broken in their song "For God Is With Us." Jon Reddick notes in his song "I Believe It (The Life of Jesus)" that Jesus does not just represent a story, but is instead an embodied, breathing, walking testimony of the goodness of God. However, each of these acknowledgements of the embodied nature of the incarnation is set within songs that employ

---

May 18, 2024, https://www.klove.com/about-us/mission.) It seems that, based on the content and the form of the media itself, exchanging the word *have* with the word *experience* might represent a more accurately articulated mission statement.

that notion to emphasize the meanings of more abstract notions like the goodness, holiness, grace, and love of God.

In addition, even when artists refer to their own bodies and their own practices, they are not the song's central focus and used as a means of considering more spiritual or theological ideas. Here we see Jeremy Camp in his song "Anxious Heart" singing of the way he experiences anxiety in his body, documenting his racing heart, shaking hands, and lost breath. However, the description of his embodied experience is constructed to serve his description of the metaphorical light that he experiences in his dark moments, and the ways he believes his experience of divine love calms his anxious heart. The emphasis on the abstract as the intended center of the lyric can be seen in Camp's use of the body to describe his anxiety. Here the body simply represents the space in which anxiety is experienced. There is no sense that the body represents a good in itself. In addition, he does not follow up to describe the way calm or peace are experienced in his body.[59] Within the form, or perhaps better the narrative pattern of these songs, abstract notions such as love, grace, and holiness typically represent a greater good than any experience rooted in the particularity of the body.[60]

This framing of the body primarily as a means to express the experience of divine or ecstatic encounters can also be heard in the words of the DJs that encourage the listener toward these ends. In a video posted to YouTube, DJ Lauree, who is expanding on a listener's testimony that K-Love had prevented her from committing

59 While Camp does note in the last chorus that God represents life when his breath is gone, he does not linger, immediately referring to the experience of being stuck in a metaphorical storm.

60 In another example, TobyMac also refers to embodied experiences in his song "Cornerstone." He opens his song singing about looking out his window and later sings of sweating through a long night because of experiences of shame. However, the song uses these and the descriptions of other less embodied, more internalized, experiences to emphasize that they matter less to Mac that the experience of God as his metaphorical cornerstone. In each of these the body is employed as a means of getting to articulate the importance of the abstract notions the represent the main idea that the artist desires to point the listener to.

suicide, notes, "Don't take it for granted that that song that came on that spoke to your heart in such a profound way, that is God's gift to you . . . because you are so precious to God."[61] She goes on to note, "What you're experiencing here at K-Love is a beautiful expression of God's love for you."[62] The emphasis here, as in the songs, is on the listener's experience of divine encounter through the practice of listening to the station.

Interestingly, even when DJ's call listeners toward other bodily practices, they are also often framed in terms of the listener's experience, and even personal benefit. For example, in a YouTube short DJ Carlos calls on K-Love listeners to join a small group, which is a smaller subset of a church community that meets together for the purposes of encouragement, fellowship, or participation in particular practices or ministries. However, he frames his reasons for encouraging the listener toward these practices entirely in terms of the experiential benefit of the listener. He notes, "There's a reason God calls us to live in community, because together we can be made stronger. When you're feeling weak, your friend, your family, someone in a small group can help lift you up."[63] He goes on to recall, "It's in my small group that I've learned a lot about myself, and a lot about my faith."[64] Note that this embodied practice is framed as for the benefit of the experience of the listener, as opposed to framing this also as a practice in service to the other participants in the small group. This emphasis on the body as a type of vehicle for internal, even emotional, experiences speaks to the emotively embodied experiential imagination and disposition that represents the ongoing aesthetic formation among K-Love listeners.

---

61 K-Love, "God Saved a Listener's Life through a Song on K-Love: Lauree Reacts," YouTube, posted April 26, 2022, accessed May 18, 2024, https://www.youtube.com/watch?v=WBWLFco96Tw&t=41s, 1:01.

62 K-Love, "God Saved a Listener's Life," 1:45.

63 K-Love, "Carlos on How Being a Part of a Small Group Impacted His Life," YouTube, posted June 21, 2023, accessed May 18, 2024, https://www.youtube.com/shorts/JcU8HklWeq0.

64 K-Love, "Carlos on How Being a Part."

The formation of this imagination and these dispositions can be further seen in listeners' descriptions of their practices in their testimonies. In each of these testimonies, the affection for the experience of listening to the music and testimonies on K-Love directly funds their continued listening to K-Love, which then represents a core devotional practice. In each instance, the emotively embodied experience of K-love's worship songs and testimonies, in both musical and propositional forms, represents the center of their affections for K-Love and the reason they continue to employ their bodies for the practice of listening. The listener who secretly tuned her husband's car radio to K-Love and who was successful in encouraging listening habits that included K-Love says, "When we sing together that's just awesome and to have that in my relationship is just unbelievable."[65] Note that while the listener exhibits a strong desire for her husband to listen to K-Love, her desire is framed around her experience of her relationship; the notion that this experience of singing these songs she loves with her husband represents an aesthetic experience that seems to have embodied a narrative she had grown to love. Notice as well that she does not speak explicitly about any notions regarding his faith or conversion. Employing the testimonial template of moving from darkness to light, it might even seem implicit that the husband's practice of listening to K-Love might by itself constitute a full experience of conversion. In any case, the emphasis in her testimony is on her experience.

These listening and service practices that are funded by affections for an emotively embodied experience of divine encounter are themselves rooted in the aesthetic texts broadcast by K-Love, represented deeply meaningful and robust practices that are fundamental to many of the listener's senses of well-being. While the practices may seem unpretentious, they are not experienced by the listener as thin. Recall listener Jack's recollection of the role K-Love played in helping him to navigate the loss of his wife to cancer: "Without those songs

---

65 K-Love, "K-Love Listener Story—How Great Is Our God," YouTube, March 28, 2013, https://youtu.be/oG37tI8u-IM?si=OXxbQiDxTiy9ANnA, 0:27.

picking my up, I could have easily caved in."[66] He goes on to recall, "That constant feed, that Sunday sermon that my Jesus was with me all day long just, you know, gave me the strength to get through."[67] K-Love includes many testimonies like these on their YouTube channel as well, documenting people's experiences of how the aesthetic texts of K-Love helped them to navigate their own moments of physical, emotional, and spiritual distress or anxiety. In each of these instances however listeners are pointed toward a particular range of practices (listening, service, and giving) that represent specific visions of Christian discipleship rooted in practices that express an authentic set of emotive embodiments that dramatically render an affectively formed inner life by means of K-Love's aesthetic texts.

Meaning Making and Narrative

The practice of listening to K-Love alongside the practices of giving and acts of service and kindness that grow out of listening also represent individual and community projects of meaning making and narrative creation. K-Love, like OCC, is itself a large-scale project in meaning making, broadcasting particularly Evangelical sets of meanings and narratives into the world for the sole purpose of growing affections for, persuading minds toward, and encouraging practices that enact its evangelically flavored sets of meanings and narratives. To describe the relationship between K-Love's aesthetics and the practices they fund, the narratives are generally embedded in each type of song and create the meaning that K-Love's listeners make of these narratives which are then dramatically rendered into action in their practices.

The worship songs of K-Love's top thirty songs of 2022 and 2023 provide a snapshot of the aesthetic formation among K-Love listeners. These curated songs share common concepts, such as grace, holiness, salvation, and sin. These notions employed in these songs

66 K-Love, "How a K-Love Listener Found Hope," 0:50.
67 K-Love, "How a K-Love Listener Found Hope," 0:58.

become more of an ambiguous shorthand, or perhaps a devotional nod or a type of musical hyperlink, to more robust theological dialogues and poetic utterances. These song's writers emphasize the internal experience of these concepts while they also then hide the human body in the narratives of these songs. They also emphasize the ecstatic experience of the meaning of the songs in the embodied practices of worship, offering a type of worship two-step as it relates to the meaning afforded the body. The songs' emphases on the internalization of these ideas in the listener's affections and imaginations offer a snapshot of the meanings its listeners make of these musical narratives.

As an example of the latter emphasis on spiritual, perhaps even disembodied, articulations of these theological ideas, recall Phil Wickham's anthemic "This Is Our God." He asks the listener to remember their experience of the walls of sin and shame, noting that Jesus's death and resurrection rendered those walls rubble. He then asks the listener to remember the giants of death and the grave, noting that they are themselves dead now. He finally calls in the listener to remember that this is who God is, the one who saves. He goes on in the bridge to ask who pulled him out of that pit, asserting that Jesus did. While notions of sin, shame, and death may be universal to the human experience in some ways, with meanings taking on different shades in different contexts, cultures, Christian denominations, and religions, Wickham here seems to be assuming a great deal of familiarity with the specifically Evangelical manner in which he is using the words in these songs. This allows him to draw on the depth of their meaning as they are likely already embedded in the listener's imagination without a great deal of work to contextualize these significant theological notions. He also uses metaphorical imagery to allow the listener to feel the emotive weight of the words, placing them alongside the weight these words already held in the listener's imagination. For example, he associates sin and shame with prison and the giants of death and the grave with mountains, later availing the notion of an altar in the wilderness to allow the listener to feel the significance of God's faithfulness.

Wickham goes on to note that these metaphorical images reveal who God is by means of what God does, which is to save "us" by the power of the cross, again assuming a significant level of listener familiarity with the Gospel narratives. This emphasis on the effect of the cross without a nod to the embodied work on the cross distances the embodiment necessary for its significance from the meaning Wickham is asking the listener to make of that event. In all of this, Wickham steers the listener away from the physical, embodied realities that are necessarily a part of the expression of these ideas toward the affective experience of the meanings of these ideas. Here the interior experience represents the primary reason for the song.

There is a similar emphasis on a disembodied interiority in the text Brandon Lake's song "Gratitude." In the song he notes that he uses his body to throw up his hands and praise God, but then goes on to note that he has nothing fit for a king except a heart singing hallelujah. Note that Lake believes a heart singing hallelujah is fit for a king, but does not articulate a value for the body, even as uses his voice to sing while raising his hands with enthusiasm in the video for this song. Even in the bridge where he calls on his soul to abandon its shyness and praise the Lord, it is his soul and not his body that he sings has a lion in its lungs. This tension in how the body is framed appears front and center here. The song emphasizes the internal experiences of worship, and marginalizes the body in its narrative, while the singer uses his body with abandon to dramatically render those internal affections visible and audible. In all of this, privilege is given to the authentic experience of the divine, framing the use of the body as an expression of that internal reality. In both examples, that experience is framed as the raison d'etre for these songs intended for worship. Both the narrative instantiated in the songs highlight the importance of the authentic experience of worship and the embodied expressions of that worship work hand-in-hand to form the affections, imaginations, and dispositions of the Evangelicals who listen to K-Love. The same is true, though employing a different set of narratives, for the K-Love's songs of testimony.

The songs that K-Love broadcasts that can be identified as testimonial songs do their work of forming affections, imaginations, and dispositions a little differently. They do this by offering a template for individual's and community's constructions of narratives intended to make sense of their lives in the light of their faith in Jesus. These narratives tend to share a common trajectory, following the one sharing the story through song from some type of darkness to the light represented by Jesus. This trajectory from darkness to light can take different forms. For example, moving from striving to rest—that is from the effort to achieve some spiritual or even a material goal, trusting in one's work for the desired outcome, to a type of resting trust that the individual can trust God for the outcome. Other like trajectories include from need to provision, or from brokenness to wholeness. With each, the narrative trajectory laid out in the songs is that this set of trajectories represents the normative expectation for the circumstances of the person Christian.

This trajectory appears in the Cody Carnes song "Ain't Nobody." He begins his song noting that he was a wandering blind man until he saw the light. In this song the light that drew him out of the darkness is the notion that nobody loves him like Jesus. He goes on to share the experience of freedom this provides for him. A similar trajectory in the Jordan St. Cyr song "Weary Traveler." The song speaks in the second person, addressing the listener directly. St. Cyr writes of the listener's experiences of weariness and restlessness. He goes on to note that they were not intended to make their way through life alone and encourages the listener to allow Jesus to carry their burdens. These songs instantiate this testimonial template well, narrating a type of normative story shape for the Evangelical Christian's life, allowing the listener to self-narrate their own experiences into the trajectories of these musical stories.

Alongside this narrative trajectory there is another set of narrative expectations embedded in these songs. Here the singer also shares their experience of moving from vulnerability to security, with the emphasis being on a type of interior, spiritual security that may at times manifest itself in material reality as well. This appears in Blanca and Tauren Well's song "Something Better." They sing of the experience of being on their own and losing loved ones along the way, but also note that they felt assured that they were safe because of "You." They further note that "You" reconstruct the broken pieces of people's lives, and that "You" are the source of the listener's new narrative. Note that that "Something Better" is left for the listener to fill in. Brandon Heath shares something similar in his song "See Me through It." He notes that he trusts God will see him through experiences of trial and pain, further noting later in the song that God is the only one who knows how to solve his problems, even if he is at his "rock bottom." Again, even as one can expect to experience vulnerability, the narrative expectation set here is that the normative experience that accompanies trust in Jesus is that of spiritual security that may also be rendered as a material reality as well.

Each of these testimony narratives also share with the worship songs an emphasis on the affective experiences of the singers and listeners. It is these affective narratives that shape the ways in which K-Love listeners perceive the world around them: their church, their neighbors, their coworkers. The privilege given to narratives of affective spiritual experience goes on to shape the narrative meaning many make of their own experiences and the experiences of their friends and neighbors. It is these narratives that get enacted in the practices that are funded by these narratives among K-Love listeners.

K-LOVE AND EVANGELICAL FORMATION

K-Love's aesthetic texts and practices offer insight into the narratives and projects of meaning making that form Evangelical affections and imaginations, and the way they perceive the world. The aesthetics form Evangelical dispositions and practices, through a deeply embedded affection for emotionally embodied experiences of divine encounter rooted in what are often lyrically abstracted theological notions such as love, grace, and holiness. The practice of listening to and singing these songs about these ideas, and what they mean for and to the individual, represents one that is deeply loved. However, the affective experience of what these words mean to the listener seems to be privileged over their denotative meanings. The experience of divine love, grace, and mercy becomes privileged over the semantic depths instantiated in those words. Also privileged is the affection for narratives of triumph and victory over life's difficulties and narrative story arcs that carry the listener from darkness to light.

K-Love's aesthetic texts and practices fund Evangelicals' loves, and the practices that rise out of those loves. A love for personal affective experiences and practices make those experiences possible, rooted in Pentecostal and Charismatic devotional and liturgical dispositions and practices.

CHAPTER 7

Film Watching as a Spiritual, Aesthetic, and Ethically Formational Practice

> This movie gave me chills as I continued to watch and no lie, when they were telling others to spread the message, "God's Not Dead" I took out my cell phone as well and began to text others the same message because the movie was just that powerful to me. You get this sense of emotion that comes over you and you know it's real! I was so not expecting this movie to do that. I am a believer in God and very proud of it.
>
> —JoJo, reviewer on Amazon, "Wonderful MUST See Movie!"

Evangelicals have been involved in filmmaking for the entire history of film as a means of proclaiming the gospel. At the same time, Evangelicals have harbored a love/hate relationship with Hollywood and the institutions that create popular films. Because of the way film can persuade affections, Evangelicals have felt conflicted; film can both lead audiences astray from their Evangelical devotional commitments and can be used to aid in the broad evangelization of American culture. Because of the power film instantiates to shape the imaginations, dispositions, and practices of its viewers, Evangelicals' relationship with the institutions that create movies is rooted in the recognition of film's ability to shape the audience's affections for both good and ill.

Evangelical filmmakers hope to form the affections, imaginations, and practices of their audiences toward a particular Evangelical Christianity–shaped vision of the good life and Christian identity. Theologian and film historian J. Ryan Parker writes that Evangelicals' relationship to film can be thought of in three ways: in the representations of Christianity in film (both as it relates to its scriptural narratives and to the stories of the lives of its followers), in the role Christians play in the institutions that produce films, and in the creative work of specifically Christian film productions.[1] In what follows here, the focus will be squarely on the third of these Evangelical relationships to film. To that end, that focus will fall on two films that represent specifically Christian film productions, intended to affectively form the imaginations, affections, dispositions, and practices of their audiences: the 2008 Sherwood Pictures film *Fireproof*, and the 2014 Pure Flix Entertainment film *God's Not Dead*. As a set of Evangelical aesthetic texts, each has played a part in the formation of Evangelical affections, dispositions, and practices in the twenty-first century.

EVANGELICAL FILMMAKING AS MEANING MAKING

Evangelicals often create cultural institutions and practices that parallel their secular counterparts. Dating back to the onset of film as a medium in the late nineteenth century, Christians have employed film as a means of creating affective experiences intended to evangelize, encourage, and exhort its audience. J. Ryan Parker notes that in addition to those parallel tracks, almost every technological advance

1 J. Ryan Parker, *Cinema as Pulpit: Sherwood Pictures and the Church Film Movement* (McFarland & Co, 2012), 17.

in filmmaking has been marked by religious films, with Evangelicals employing each technological advancement in film and sound as a means of more aesthetically and affectively buoying their proclamation of the gospel.[2] This earnest impulse is at play in many of Hollywood's classic "Sandal and Robe" films rooted in various biblical narratives such as Cecil B. DeMille's 1927 *King of Kings*, his 1956 epic *The Ten Commandments*, Henry Koster's 1953 film *The Robe*, and William Wyler's 1959 film *Ben Hur*. A revival of that earnest impulse is present in Mel Gibson's 2004 *The Passion of the Christ*.

With the collapse of the studio system in Hollywood alongside the end of the Catholic-influenced production codes in the mid-1960s, films whose subject matter were religion broadly and Christianity specifically were able to adopt a more critical point of view in their filmmaking, mirroring much of the broader culture's own impulses.[3] Evangelicals however never wavered in their endeavors to create films that shared the tenets of their faith and therefore took up the mantle of creating these films themselves, independent of the Hollywood studios. Evangelicals were creating aesthetic texts that more consistently instantiated the doctrinal and devotional commitments that were embedded in their broader meaning-making projects. They took up this mantle because the manner in which Evangelicals constructed meaning from film (and other aesthetic texts) was different than the ways in which aesthetic meaning was constructed by the wider popular culture. Evangelical meaning was constructed within a particular culture of Evangelical perception.

---

2 Parker, *Cinema as Pulpit*, 5. In this way Christian films represented an extension of the dramatic and narrative impulses that gave rise the European medieval passion plays.

3 Parker, *Cinema as Pulpit*, 5. Parker notes that this more critical impulse can be seen at play in films like Martin Scorsese's 1988 film *The Last Temptation of Christ*, and DreamWorks Animation's 1998 film *The Prince of Egypt*. I would suggest better examples might be Mel Brooks's 1979 film *The History of the World, Part 1* and the British comedy troop Monty Python's 1981 film *The Life of Brian*.

The Christian films created by Evangelicals represent a complex web of meaning making, often in competition with one another. For example, the films made by Evangelicals have historically promoted a particular Evangelical understanding of concepts in the Gospels. The films are intended convert and form faith. These types of films simultaneously fulfill another purpose as well: serving to reinforce the faith of its Evangelical audience.

As these films stand in as a type of faith reinforcement, they then instantiate a set of cultural commitments that are created to sit in tension with the popular culture. Framed within a more contemporary framework, these films become a brand. They instantiate their own visual culture and cultural shorthand.[4] Those who work to create the shapes and social markers of this brand often highlight the differences between Evangelicals' and the broader culture's senses of how social, devotional, and political commitments ought to be shaped.[5]

This collective sense of brand and identity, to the extent that it is highlighted and embraced, can enhance the larger Evangelical sense of separation from the broader senses of popular and American cultures. Films then become not only endeavors to persuade the audience toward spiritual conversion, but also represent a portion of a social-aesthetic commitment to convert the members of the broader culture toward a particular set of social and political dispositions, absent of the intended spiritual conversion. Something of this social

4 Parker quotes Richard Lindsay as he argues that Evangelical films represent something akin to subculture filmmaking, or filmmaking that is rooted in ethnic identities. He notes specifically of the Evangelical film studio Sherwood, "What Sherwood is doing in making this kind of independent film is the same thing small-time gay, or ethnic, or women filmmakers have been trying to do in countering the dominant narrative that Hollywood creates" (172).

5 These markers of difference have been highlighted over the years with varying degrees of rivalry. Viewed from the perspective of Evangelical films, these tensions represent humble appeals to the Evangelical faith and the Evangelical vision of how the world ought to be, but they can also represent a vision of fundamental dissimilarity and even conflict, leading to a more combative disposition and what is often framed as the "culture wars."

and political disposition can be seen in the words of director Alex Kendrick, recorded in behind-the-scenes footage on the first day of the filming of *Fireproof*: "Today is the first day we go to war, and we're going to take some ground."[6] While this type of bellicose language has often been employed aesthetically by Evangelicals toward broadly spiritual ends, this approach is easily entwined with the social and political as well.[7] The ground Kendrick is endeavoring to take back is likely as much cultural ground as it is spiritual.

FILM #1: *FIREPROOF*

Fireproof was produced by Sherwood Pictures, a studio created by Sherwood Baptist Church in Albany, Georgia. *Fireproof* was the third film produced by the studio/ministry, following the films *Flywheel* and *Facing the Giants*. It was directed by Alex Kendrick. The film's protagonist is Caleb Holt, played by Kirk Cameron, a professional fire captain in Albany. The film's narrative is built around his dissolving marriage to Catherine Holt, played by Erin Bethea, a public affairs director at a local hospital. Early on, the film establishes both Caleb's dream to buy a boat, for which he is saving money, and his mother-in-law's need for in-home medical equipment following a debilitating stroke. During an early quarrel in the film, Catherine accuses Caleb of selfishness and confronts him regarding his habit of regularly watching internet pornography. Caleb physically threatens her, and Catherine tearfully asks for a divorce, to which Caleb angrily agrees.

Caleb discusses these events with his friend, a fellow firefighter, Lt. Michael Simmons, played by Alex Bevel, and his father John

6 Quoted in Parker, *Cinema as Pulpit*, 88.

7 Examples of the bellicosity embedded in Evangelical aesthetic texts would include hymns such as "Onward Christian Soldiers," "The Battle Hymn of the Republic," and "Soldiers of Christ, Arise." We could also include the children's Sunday school song "I'm in the Lord's Army."

Holt, played by Harris Malcom. Both council him to hold off on agreeing to the divorce, with his father giving him a forty-day challenge that he calls The Love Dare. Caleb agrees but does not tell Catherine what he is doing. Each day The Love Dare directs the reader to practice a different challenge. For example, the first challenge tasks the reader to utter no unkind words to their spouse, even if that means remaining silent. Caleb follows the daily challenges, but finds them difficult, particularly in light of Catherine's consistent suspicion of and rejection of his overtures. At the same time as Caleb's attempt to complete The Love Dare, Catherine is maintaining an ongoing office flirtation with Dr. Gavin Keller, played by Perry Revell.

About halfway through The Love Dare, Caleb's father shares with Caleb that much of the difficulty he is experiencing in his attempts to repursue Catherine is rooted in his fundamental misunderstanding of love, encouraging Caleb to an evangelically shaped faith in Jesus Christ, to which Caleb assents. This scene represents the film's raison d'etre. Aside from the film's emphasis on the importance of marriage, it also exists to persuade the audience to their own personal conversions. Soon after Caleb's conversion he secretly uses the money he had set aside for his boat to pay for the medical equipment needed by his mother-in-law. He also learns of the doctor's pursuit of Catherine and confronts him in his office. Following the confrontation, the doctor ends his flirtation with Catherine.

In the final set of scenes Catherine learns of The Love Dare and learns that Caleb is beyond the forty days prescribed by the dare but is still practicing its directives. Caleb offers a heartfelt apology for his actions that hurt and diminished her; however, she indicates she still needs time to consider the divorce, to which Caleb agrees. Catherine soon learns that Caleb was the individual who had paid $24,000 for his mother-in-law's medical equipment, believing it had been Dr. Keller. Moved by Caleb's grand gesture, she reconciles with him. The film ends with a renewal of Caleb's and Catherine's wedding vows. In the film, this second commitment is described as a covenant under the auspices of their shared faith in Christ.

The Aesthetic Highlights of *Fireproof*

Film as a medium is adept at instantiating myriad layers of meaning at once. To understand the ways in which *Fireproof* works to form the affections, dispositions, and practices of its audience, one must attend to these layers of meaning. The first is the role an Evangelical understanding of marriage plays in the formation of its audience's affections. Undergirding the film's broadly Evangelical understanding of marriage lies an essentialist understanding of masculinity and femininity.[8] For example, Lt. Simmons offers this marriage advice to Caleb: "But just remember—a woman's like a rose: if you treat her right, she'll bloom; if you don't, she'll wilt."[9] Conversely, a nurse and colleague of Catherine asserts in a later conversation, "A real man's got to be a hero to his wife before he can be to anybody else, or he ain't a real man."[10] Each character articulates culturally embedded yet universally framed understandings of gender and sex that then play out in the ways in which Lt. Simmons and Caleb's father frame their advice for Caleb regarding his marriage.[11] These cultural com-

8 By essentialist, I mean the aesthetic and doctrinal commitment that masculinity and femininity are ontologically attached to the body of the individual and not conditionally rooted in the cultural iterations or understandings of each. It is the commitment that the definitions of masculinity and femininity are universally fixed across the human experience and cannot be changed by human cultural constructs.

9 *Fireproof*, directed by Alex Kendrick (Sherwood Pictures, 2008), 7:46.

10 *Fireproof*, 13:09

11 It must be noted that these aesthetic articulations are consistent with the most recent Baptist Faith and Message, released in 2000. Section XVIII notes, "The husband and wife are of equal worth before God, since both are created in God's image. The marriage relationship models the way God relates to His people. A husband is to love his wife as Christ loved the church. He has the God-given responsibility to provide for, to protect, and to lead his family. A wife is to submit herself graciously to the servant leadership of her husband even as the church willingly submits to the headship of Christ. She, being in the image of God as is her husband and thus equal to him, has the God-given responsibility to respect her husband and to serve as his helper in managing the household and nurturing the next generation." See Baptist Faith and Message 2000, The Baptist Faith and Message, accessed July 22, 2024, https://bfm.sbc.net/bfm2000/#xviii.

mitments become embedded in the aesthetics of the film. In turn, they represent a portion of the vision of the good life that that the filmmakers embed in the audience's affections and imagination.

The next layers of meaning are the visual and narrative embedding of the male gaze, and particularly the white male gaze.[12] This layer runs directly adjacent to and even overlaps the film's aesthetic commitment to an essentialism masculinity and femininity. British film critic and theorist Laura Mulvey uses the gaze to describe what she perceives to be a primarily male-centric image-creating construct in filmmaking. She suggested films are historically made primarily from the perspective of a male subject, which commonly sees women as objects of desire. Thus, films tend to codify the cultural gender constructs of men as actively looking and women as being passively looked at.[13] The instantiation of a form of this gaze, which literally represents the lens through which the audience is led to view and perceive the images and narrative of the film, also represents a portion of the filmmaker's aesthetic commitments that are embedded in the film. This commitment to viewing the characters and narrative of the film from the perspective of the male subject is visible in the same conversations cited earlier with Lt. Simmons and Catherine's colleague. Because these aesthetic commitments are embedded in *Fireproof*'s images and narrative, they also represent a portion of the aesthetic processes working to form the audience's affections and imaginations.

The next layer of meaning is Caleb's conversion story. While this arc represents a central component of the larger narrative the directors are creating, instantiating the moment Caleb came to truly

12 The notion of the male gaze can be traced to French psychologist Jacques Lacan's notion of the gaze, which represents the understanding that the individual is also an object visible to others. The notion of the gaze was previously engaged with David Morgan's use of this idea in his description of the aesthetically formational power of the Evangelical gaze.

13 See Laura Mulvey, "Visual Pleasure and Narrative Cinema," *Screen*, 16, no. 3 (Autumn 1975), accessed July 22, 2024, https://ia802801.us.archive.org/4/items/visual-pleasure-and-narrative-cinema/Laura-mulvey-visual-pleasure-and-narrative-cinema.pdf.

understand the nature of love, deepening his commitment to and the meaning that he assigned to and received from The Love Dare, it seems to be handled with less clarity then one might expect, especially considering the evangelistic intentions of the film. The film promotes the Evangelical understanding of salvation. In addition, Caleb's rejection of God's love is juxtaposed with Catherine's rejection of Caleb's love, forcing Caleb to consider the ways in which his spiritual condition might relate to his crumbling marriage. Even with the film's assertion that Caleb will not be able to love his wife properly without understanding and imitating the self-giving love embodied by Jesus, Caleb's salvation appears as a type of panacea that leads directly to the film's ultimate happy ending, a type of Evangelical deus ex machina that inevitably achieves the requisite end of the couple's reconciliation. Space does not appear to be given to the notion that, even within this Evangelical set of theological commitments, not everyone requites the love of God with their own faith and love. There appears to be no narrative sense that Caleb's assent to faith here was not inevitable.[14]

These are only a handful of the aesthetic commitments embedded in *Fireproof*, but they represent some of the most important. They represent the seeds that shape affections and imaginations.

FILM #2: *GOD'S NOT DEAD*

God's Not Dead was produced by Pure Flix Entertainment, a company founded in 2005 for the purpose of creating Evangelical Christian films, and directed by Harold Cronk.[15] The company's website describes themselves as "a theatrical company with a passion for

14 Similarly, the success of The Love Dare also seems like a fait accompli, as if Caleb were following the directions in something like a car repair manual, repairing a marriage as one might a dead battery. The reality of the messiness of marriage of course is far more complex to be reduced in this way.

15 Pure Flix Entertainment changed its name to Pinnacle Peak Pictures in January of 2021.

influencing the culture for Jesus Christ through media."[16] They have produced all four films in the *God's Not Dead* series, along with the films *Do You Believe?*, *Woodlawn*, *The Case for Christ*, and *Unplanned*. The film *God's Not Dead* centers on Christian college student Josh Wheaton, played by Shane Harper.[17] Josh and his girlfriend Kara, played by Cassidy Gifford, arrive for their first semester at fictitious Hadley University, a stand-in for a large state-run university. Josh enrolls in an introductory philosophy course against the advice of the school employee completing his registration, who had noted the cross he was wearing on his necklace. Upon arriving to the class Josh is asked along with the rest of his fellow students to sign a statement affirming that God is dead by his assertively atheistic philosophy professor, Dr. Radisson, played by Kevin Sorbo. As a committed Christian, Josh resists signing such a statement. As an alternative, Dr. Radisson notes that if Josh cannot sign such a statement, he must defend the thesis that God exists from the podium in front of the class. This endeavor, which the professor asserts will fail, would represent 30 percent of his final grade. Josh's girlfriend orders Josh to sign the statement for the sake of their future together, noting that a poor grade could jeopardize his ability to pursue law school. However, Josh feels that "God wants someone to defend him."[18] After much soul-searching, including a conversation with a local pastor, who directs him to read Matthew 10:32–33, Josh does not relent and decides to make his case for the existence of God over the next three sessions of the class.[19] When Josh's girlfriend learns of his choice she ends their relationship.

---

16 Billy Hallowell, "Support Pure Flix and Our Mission—Here's Who We Are," Great American Pure Flix Insider, December 8, 2020, accessed July 23, 2024, https://www.pureflix.com/insider/support-pureflix-and-our-mission.

17 The character's name appears to be an obvious homage to the Christian college by the same name.

18 *God's Not Dead*, directed by Harold Cronk, (Pure Flix Entertainment, 2014), 17:11.

19 Matthew 10:32–33 reads, "Whoever acknowledges me before others, I will also acknowledge before my Father in heaven. But whoever disowns me before others, I will disown before my Father in heaven" (NIV).

Over the first two sessions Josh employs cosmological and scientific arguments for the existence of God and appears to be winning over the class. In the meantime, the film undertakes several subplots, including Dr. Radisson's relationship with Mina, an Evangelical Christian, played by Cory Oliver, and his cruel treatment of her in front of his colleagues. The film also focuses on Mina's care of her mother, who is suffering from dementia, and her relationship with her ambitious brother Mark, played by Dean Cain, a financial executive with questionable ethics. To highlight his lack of virtue, the film shows him breaking up with his girlfriend Amy, a cynical atheist reporter played by Trisha LaFache, when he learns she has cancer. Yet another subplot focuses on Reverand Dave, played by David A. R. White (one of the founders of Pure Flix Entertainment) and his attempts to take a road trip with visiting missionary Reverand Jude, played by Benjamin A. Onyango. The film also tells the story of Ayisha, played by Hadeel Sittu, a girl from a Muslim family who is banished from her family when her father learns of her conversion to Christianity. Finally, the film shows Martin Yip, played by Paul Kwo, a student visiting from China who is told by his father to cease his conversations about God over the phone so that he does not jeopardize his brother's chance of studying in the United States.

In a conversation with Dr. Radisson prior to Josh's final session defending the existence of God, he learns Radisson watched his mother die of cancer when he was twelve. During this final session, Josh engages the notion of theodicy, suggesting suffering is related to free will, noting that God's intention is to eventually destroy all evils. He goes on to engage Dr. Radisson on the subject of moral absolutes, suggesting God represents a fixed point of morality. Toward the end of the debate Dr. Radisson notes that he is going to enjoy failing Josh. Josh then uses his knowledge of Radisson's childhood and asks, "Yeah, but who are you really looking to fail, professor, me, or God?"[20] He goes on to ask the professor why he hates God, to which the professor answers, "Because he took everything away

20 *God's Not Dead*, 1:24:30.

from me."[21] Josh responds to this confession by asking, "How can you hate someone if they don't exist?"[22] The class then, rendering their judgment on the outcome of the debate, one by one stands and declares almost unanimously, "God's not dead."[23]

After the class Dr. Radisson reads a letter his mother wrote to him encouraging him to continue in his faith before she passed away. After reading the letter he calls Mina and leaves to try to find her at a local Newsboys concert, a popular Evangelical rock band. On his way, he is struck by a car and seriously injured. He is attended to by Reverend Dave and Reverend Jude and affirms his faith in Jesus before he dies. The movie ends with the Newsboys congratulating Josh for standing up to Dr. Radisson from the stage in the auditorium, ending the movie singing the song "God's Not Dead."

The Aesthetic Highlights of *God's Not Dead*

The notion of the rational credibility of Christianity is one of the primary notions framing *God's Not Dead's* aesthetic commitments. While Josh may not be directly seeking the conversion of the professor and his fellow students in his rhetorical defense of the existence of God, he is hoping to create the conditions that would render that conversion a reasonable decision, both for them, and for the audience. Here truth, perhaps best framed as a set of rational propositions, appears to be afforded the greatest sense of conceptual deference, even set against and placed over notions such as mercy, empathy, goodness, and justice. This can be seen in both the film's engagement with the notion of theodicy, and in the way the film proffers a notion of salvation that privileges the good of a future, perhaps

21 *God's Not Dead*, 1:25:12.

22 *God's Not Dead*, 1:25:30.

23 The directors may have intended for the class to stand and declare God is not dead unanimously; however IMBD notes that, humorously, one actor did not stand because he was stuck in his seat. The scene was not reshot. ("God's Not Dead," IMDB, accessed July 29, 2024, https://www.imdb.com/title/tt2528814/.)

spiritual, reality over the good that salvation might offer the current material reality.

During Josh's last session defending the notion of the existence of God he addresses the problem of evil, often popularly framed in culture as one of Christianity's primary weaknesses. The problem highlights the perceived incongruity between the existence of an all-good, all-powerful God, and the existence of evil, or that which is not good. In the film Josh notes the answer is remarkably simple, suggesting evil exists because of free will.[24] He goes on to explain, "From the Christian standpoint, God tolerates evil in this world on a temporary basis so that those who love him freely will one day dwell with him in heaven free from the influence of evil, but with their free will intact. In other words, God's intention concerning evil is to one day destroy it."[25] To which Dr. Radisson responds, "Well, how convenient. One day I will get rid of all the evil in the world, but until then you just have to deal with all the war and holocausts, tsunamis, poverty, starvation, and AIDS. Have a nice life."[26] The professor makes a valid point, naming certain streams of Christianity's escapist tendencies—that is, the tendency to frame heaven as the deus ex machina rectification of all the ills experienced in the materiality of time and space. There is an inherent inconsistency in the theology that undergirds Josh's approach to his answer. Interestingly, this inconsistency is a key part of the film's aesthetic.

---

24 In a bit of what can perhaps be framed as humorous irony, Josh (and by extension the narrative of the film) lands on the same answer to this question as the 1981 Terry Gilliam film *Time Bandits* does. We must note that *Time Bandits* in no way represents itself as a Christian film. At that film's denouement, the film's young protagonist, Kevin, played by Craig Warnock, confronts the Supreme Being, played by Ralph Richardson, with the question of why evil has to exist, a question that has percolated under the surface in the film's narrative. To this question the Supreme Being answers, rather anticlimactically and absentmindedly, "I think it has something to do with free will," before immediately moving on to more pressing matters. (*Time Bandits*, directed by Terry Gilliam, [Hand Made Films, 1981], 1:47:10). To be fair, *God's Not Dead* answers the question far more earnestly.

25 *God's Not Dead*, 1:21:09.

26 *God's Not Dead*, 1:21:39.

Embedded in Josh's answers lies the privileging of the value of the life lived after death over the life lived in the materiality of time and space. As seen earlier in some of OCC's aesthetic texts, this represents a privileging of the spiritual over the material, or a devaluing of the material. This is perhaps best displayed during the film's climax with Dr. Radisson's late conversion. With no sense of sadness or loss, Reverend Jude says directly after the passing of Dr. Radisson with a smile on his face, "What happened here tonight is a cause for celebration. Pain, yes, for just a few moments. But now, think about the joy in heaven."[27] This scene is intercut with the Newsboys concert and their celebration of what is framed as Josh's faithfulness and his vindication alongside the hint of celebration for the professor's perceived academic comeuppance. This occurs literally moments after his death both chronologically and narratively and does not offer the viewer even a moment to reflect on the sadness and potential personal loss associated with his death. No consideration is given, for example, to how either Mina, who had just texted Dr. Radisson, or Josh might experience this loss. This represents the affective instantiation of these aesthetic, devotional, and even doctrinal commitments to the privileging of the spiritual over the material.

Another example of privileging the spiritual over the material lies in the film's failure to attend to the physical suffering of its characters. There are several characters facing personal hardships in the film, experiencing firsthand the effects of the problem of evil.[28] This devalu-

---

27 *God's Not Dead*, 1:47:35.

28 Writing of this narrative feature, theologian Steven Vredenburgh notes, "The existential threats these women [the characters Ayisha and Amy] face are downplayed by suggesting that their problems can be solved without any tangible offers of assistance, such as a place to stay for Ayisha, or the offer of assistance as Amy goes through treatment for her cancer" (Steven Vredenburgh, "Evangelizing Atheism: Missing the Mark in Recent Christian Film," *Christian Scholars Review*, 50, no. 1 [Fall 2020]: 72). He frames this assertion by writing, "Most often, when a character encounters suffering in the film, they are placated by a Bible verse from one of the more devout characters. When Ayisha is violently thrown out of her house by her Muslim father for converting to Christianity, she seeks out Reverend Dave for advice. And, though Reverend

ing of the material conditions of the characters is symptomatic of the same disposition toward materiality displayed in the "celebration" of Radisson's death. Theologically speaking little consideration is given the value God might ascribe to either the materiality of creation or the material conditions of the people made in God's image. These aesthetic commitments devaluing the material work to form the dispositions of the audience to the material and the spiritual as well.

A second aesthetic commitment embedded in *God's Not Dead* is its commitment to the fundamental rationality of the Christian faith. While there exists a long tradition of the rational defense of the Christian faith, the film frames the rational defense of the faith as the preferred if not normative method of establishing its truth. However, through the centuries, Christians have also relied on the lives of the saints in their efforts to highlight Christianity's credibility—living demonstrations of the social shape of the truth, including notions like mercy, love, justice, and grace. The film's focus, as it relates to Christianity's credibility, lies solely on the reasonableness of a particular set of Christian propositions, with no discernible concern about the embodied, enacted shape of the Christian's life, effectively disconnecting the truth of the Christian faith from the life of the Christian faith. This prioritization of the rational credibility of the faith represents another of the film's aesthetic commitments that shape the affections and imaginations of its audience. While the essential aesthetic commitments in these two aesthetic texts work to form the affections, perceptions, and imagination of their audiences, these texts also work to form Evangelical practices as well.

Dave does not provide her with any tangible help, she leaves smiling because Dave reminds her that she 'can do all things through Christ' (Phil. 4:13). When Amy, the blogger, tells the Newsboys she is dying of cancer, her mood is lifted when a band member quotes a few Bible verses to her and prays for God to be with her and cleanse her" (72).

EVANGELICAL FILMS, EVANGELICAL PRACTICES

Among the core commitments of the argument that undergirds this project is the notion that aesthetic texts play a fundamental role in moral formation, aiding in the formation of individuals' and communities' affections, imaginations, and dispositions—the prerational assumptions that shape their perception of the world and their being in it. These dispositions then reveal themselves in their practices.

Fireproof and Evangelical Practices

In reviewing individual's posts and reviews regarding *Fireproof*, only a relatively small percentage of reviewers (less than 10 percent) included a description of their practices in relation to the film. For those that did include the film's effect on their practices in their reviews, these can be broken down into a handful of categories: repeated viewings of the film, purchasing materials as a result of the film, broadening or augmenting their devotional practices, and promoting the film.

The practice of watching the film may seem obvious; however, it needs to be highlighted because it is an embodied practice. To that end here is a distinction between watching the film once and watching the film often, returning to it repeatedly, as one might with a devotional text, or the Scriptures themselves. Many viewers return to the film often because they enjoy it and they enjoy the meaning they make of it. One viewer identified as kingd702 writes, "Thank God for Sherwood Pictures and the Kendrick brothers. I can hardly wait for their next film."[29] This review is representative of the many viewers who find affectionate space for the films in their imagination, not only returning to them to re-view them, but to also consider the themes and messages they perceive in the film as well.[30] This love

29 Kingd702, "Story Matters More Than Anything Else," review of *Fireproof*, IMDB, May 20, 2019, accessed July 27, 2024, https://www.imdb.com/review/rw4865791/?ref_=tt_urv.

30 We must note that around a third of the reviews of the film on both IMDB and on Amazon are decidedly and often aggressively negative. The same

of watching the film, in many viewers, often spreads out into other practices, including the practice of purchasing materials as a means to aid in other associated devotional practices.

Not only does its audience enjoy the film, it returns to them because of the pleasure of its formational effect. This pleasure then is experienced both in the process of the audience's current affections and dispositions being reinforced and as a continued formation toward ends that the audience already loves and is disposed toward. The user "Mazdaprobegt" on the IMDB website writes, "But when it comes down to it, if you're married, this movie should be a must watch. As a man, I try to watch it once in a while to remind myself how to treat the love of my life."[31] The movie serves as something like a normative vision of Christian marriage for this viewer, and others like him. It serves as an aesthetic reminder of what his own marriage practices ought to imitate. The viewer is already disposed toward these affections and dispositions. The repeated watching of the film then is a practice that continues and deepens this formation.

To further serve this formation, Sherwood Studios released *The Love Dare* as a book in an effective marketing strategy alongside the release of the movie. Written by Alex Kendrick by and Stephen Kendrick, the book represents a marriage resource available to clergy and laity alike to promote the vision of marriage instantiated in the film. The book expands the influence of the film's vision, embedding it within a parallel piece of material culture. More crassly, it also represents the commodification of the film's aesthetic commitments, also providing the opportunity for additional profit for Sherwood Films. The purchase of materials, while a set of practices in itself, is typically engaged to serve other sets of practices. In this instance, the purchase of these types of materials serves to broaden the devotional

is true of *God's Not Dead*.

31 Mazdaprobegt, "To the haters . . .", review of *Fireproof*, IMDB, December 7, 2010, accessed July 27, 2024, https://www.imdb.com/review/rw2349676/?ref_=tt_urv.

practices of the individual or the community, both individually and as it relates to their marriage.

This relationship between the repeated viewing of the films and the audience's devotional practices are at play in a review from SW VA Gal, who writes, "Several of us stayed over and discussed getting the kits that go with it. The next day [after seeing *Fireproof*] I ordered enough for a class and scheduled a study group for the next two months. The kit is awesome too. Our study group used the books to help spur conversation and life changing advise [*sic*]. This was truly one of the best 'Bible' study classes I have attended."[32] The film is employed as a devotional text as it is used to facilitate discussion. In addition, the film not only shapes community devotional practices, but also private individual practices as well. An example of this comes from Kdosda_Hegen: "And besides everything, the film is very deep, it motivates me to improve upon myself and inspires me to be a better person."[33] While the viewer does not offer a detailed account of the particular practices they believe need to change in order to improve themselves into a better person, there is the acknowledgement that the film has resulted in, at the very least, a nudge of their affections, and a small change in their practices. In each of these cases, however, there is a glimpse of the manner in which the film inspires a change in the viewer's affections and imagination that results in some change in their devotional practices.

Finally, there is the practice of promoting the film. Many of those who have developed an affection for *Fireproof* show that affection by attempting to persuade prospective viewers to see the film themselves, offering myriad arguments and benefits for the viewing. As an example, "pastormlmueller" writes in a review, "I used to work

32 SW VA Gal, "Excellent Film for Couples!," review of *Fireproof*, Amazon, February 15, 2010, accessed July 27, 2024, https://www.amazon.com/gp/customer-reviews/R2V3QU0NSUH978/.

33 Kdosda_Hegen, "If You Don't Mind Christian Themes and Pretty Low Production Values, Definitely Give This One a Try," review of *Fireproof*, IMDB, August 22, 2023, accessed July 27, 2024, https://www.imdb.com/review/rw9276891/?ref_=tt_urv.

in Hollywood and now serve as a pastor in West Texas. This movie has excellent production values and an excellent message (despite its decision theology underpinnings—not very Biblical). Please go and see this movie and bring your loved one and your teens and all of your family."[34] The role Evangelical films represent as a marker of Evangelical identity and something like a faith brand is visible here. This pastor endorses the potential aesthetically formational role this film could play in its audience's lives, even as he is critical of what he perceives as a conflict between a personal doctrinal commitment and the film's fundamental doctrinal commitments.[35] Here, it appears the pastor values the importance of the Evangelical brand over doctrinal particularities. What is being promoted is as much about the validity and credibility of that brand as it is about the particular content of the film.

The promotional commitment to the Evangelical brand also comes into play in the review of msstafford8, as she writes, "Bringing the ideals and mindful caring that is missing in this world today to life as this film did will always be with me. We should send a copy to every troop fighting across the way. God Bless family and god bless America. Amen."[36] In any case, whether promoting the film because

34 Pastorlmueller, "Excellent Movie for Couples and Singles Alike!," review of *Fireproof*, IMDB, September 4, 2008, accessed July 27, 2024, https://www.imdb.com/review/rw1940704/?ref_=tt_urv.

35 This pastor's criticism of the film's "decision theology" is rooted in what is likely this pastor's Reformed theological commitments. Decision theology represents the theological understanding that an individual's salvation is directly tied to their affirmative decision to accept or follow Christ. Historically, this theological disposition would be more common within Baptist and Methodist churches. Reformed theology tends to view the faith that results in salvation as a gift in and of itself; thus the individual is not actually making an affirmative decision to accept or follow Jesus. Instead, their decision is the result of a divine gift. A helpful introductory account of these different approaches to these theological commitments can be found in chapters 4, 6, and 7 of W. David Buschart, *Exploring Protestant Traditions: An Invitation to Theological Hospitality* (IVP Academic, 2006).

36 Msstafford8, "A Must See," review of *Fireproof*, IMDB, March 4, 2014, accessed July 27, 2024, https://www.imdb.com/review/rw2979608/?ref_=tt_urv.

of the aesthetic and devotional contents of the film or promoting the film as an instantiation of the Evangelical brand, the film aesthetically engages the individual promoter's imagination and affections to the extent that they want to share the pleasure and the positive effects they have experienced with others through their promotion. Interestingly, similar practices flow from the viewing of *God's Not Dead*; however, there is a unique set of practices that spring directly out of that film's content that differ from the practices funded by *Fireproof*.[37]

God's Not Dead and Evangelical Practices

Before directly engaging the audience practices funded by the repeated viewing of *God's Not Dead*, I wanted to quickly note the different contexts into which these two films were released. *God's Not Dead* was released in 2014, six years after *Fireproof's* 2008 release. As Kristin Kobes du Mez documents in her book *Jesus and John Wayne*, Evangelicalism experienced significant changes in that period. *Fireproof* was released at the end of what Kobes Du Mez might call the Tender Warrior period between the late 1990s and the middle 2000s, characterized by the cultural and theological commitments of The Promise Keeper's ministry.[38] The film reflects the broadly less belligerent disposition among Evangelicals, and among white Evangelical males in particular, during this period. *God's Not Dead*, on the other

37 I also want to briefly note that Evangelicals are not the only ones who promote the perceived virtues of *Fireproof*. Among the reviews on Amazon was one by a Catholic viewer who wrote, "A priest assigned watching this as a penance in Confession once and I've loved it ever since. Every time I feel like I've been a mediocre husband recently I watch this, and it inspires me to do better." (Phil T., "One of My Favorites," review of *Fireproof*, Amazon, February 4, 2024, accessed July 27, 2024, https://www.amazon.com/gp/customer-reviews/R3BJ0FBE9R9TR3/.

38 "Tender Warriors" is the title of her chapter that addresses this period. Kobes Du Mez notes that within this timeframe within Evangelicalism the notion that men should balance "traditional masculine authority and a defense of an emotive, egalitarian, reconstructed Christian manhood" became a popular cultural disposition (153).

hand, was released in the middle of Barack Obama's second term as president, as instantiations of a more aggressive, conflict-tolerant, perhaps even conflict-seeking Evangelicalism was growing, both in the number of Evangelicals embracing this approach, and in the affections and imaginations of individuals and Evangelical communities of faith. *God's Not Dead*'s narrative and aesthetic instantiate this shift in cultural and theological dispositions within its devotional and aesthetic commitments.

As with *Fireproof*, reviewers cite their repeated watching of the film, along with promotion of the film as common practices. People also acknowledge the role the film has played in the expansion of their personal devotional practices.[39] What is unique to *God's Not Dead* is its more culturally confrontational disposition, and by extension, the embodiment of that disposition in its audience. As an example, Sherrill Murray articulates what she perceives as the films value as an instructional aid: "I find this an excellent teaching tool for young adults who may be challenged by the world they live in and intimidated by having different opinions from highly educated persons around them. It does not deal with all the questions people pose about Virgin Birth, parting of the Red Sea, etc. It simply deals with reasons to believe in God and reasons why we should not allow the highly educated teaching staff dictate such decisions in our life."[40] Running alongside the practice of using the film as a teaching tool runs the practice of defending Christianity, or framed more confrontationally, fighting for the credibility of Christianity. Indeed, the

---

39 As an example, we see shaylabnelson write, "I personally watch this movie every single day because it feels like God wants me to know that there is a movie out there where people understand my situation or share my faith in Christ. I was very pleased with this movie and this has helped reform my life into a better one" (Shaylabnelson, "This Movie Rocks!, review of *God's Not Dead*, IMDB, July 29, 20155, accessed July 27, 2024, https://www.imdb.com/review/rw3286879/?ref_=tt_urv).

40 Sherrill Murray, "Each of the Issues Could Have Easlly Taken Whole Time to Fully Explore," review of *God's Not Dead*, Amazon, September 13, 2014, accessed July 27, 2024, https://www.amazon.com/gp/customer-reviews/RSQJZKZM3BUG7/.

practices of defending Christianity against those who would seek to undermine its credibility, or indeed supplant it entirely, represents the content this film is teaching as an instructional aid.

A reviewer who identifies herself as lisafrance-25224 notes of the film's affective role in shaping both her dispositions and the practice of defending the faith, "This movie made me cry, it is so powerful down to the ending. I watched it twice, and will probably watch it a few more times to learn how to better defend my faith when questioned."[41] Another reviewer, itskervin, notes similarly on IMDB, "This movie inspired me greatly to be strong in my Faith and to defend him. For some time, its [*sic*] been difficult for me to try and defend God because of the people I surround myself with."[42] Here the film provides a dramatic enactment of what is framed within the narrative of the film as a reasoned account of the existence of God, and thus a reasoned account of the credibility of Christianity. Framed as a fundamental good, this notion of the defense of the Christian faith, in this confrontational format, becomes an affective telos of those whose dispositions are being formed toward this type of end.

In the film, while Josh's defense of the existence of God is fundamentally confrontational, it is also largely respectful of the atheist arguments he is engaging. This is true even if, at times, he makes his arguments against "straw men" of his own creation and engages in personal attacks against his professor, as in the climax of their debate.[43] Formationally, however, in the social and devotional context into which this film was released, the audience did not universally seek to engage their individual opponents, surrounding culture,

---

41 Lisafrance-25224, "I Basically Created IMDB Just to Review THIS MOVIE!! IT'S SO GOOD," review of *God's Not Dead*, IMDB, December 21, 2020, accessed July 27, 2024, https://www.imdb.com/review/rw6385579/?ref_=tt_urv.

42 Itskervin, "Beautiful Movie," review of *God's Not Dead*, IMDB, April 5, 2015, accessed July 27, 2024, https://www.imdb.com/review/rw3214936/?ref_=tt_urv.

43 To be fair, Dr. Radisson is guilty of the same offenses at different moments in the film.

or opposing viewpoints with similar respect and restraint.[44] Many viewed the film as a call to not only defend the credibility of Christianity, but to fight against those who they perceived as marginalizing their faith or belittling those who believe it.

This next level of pugnaciousness is in view in a review from Leo Hott: "We are in the middle of a second revolution both spiritually & physically as our current President [Trump] is fighting to drain the swamp of Satanist [*sic*] that were one election away from totally destroying this country!!! God is definitely NOT DEAD. . . . This movie helps bolster your faith & please pray that our living God protects all the patriots fighting so hard to pull our country out of the grips of the Luciferians trying to tear us apart!!!"[45] While the aggressiveness of this type of post is present in only a small fraction of the reviews online, they represent content written by individuals that are present and active (and loud) participants in the interpretive community of the film a community that exists almost entirely within the American Evangelical church.

AESTHETICS TO PRACTICES

To account for the aesthetic formation that occurs as people engage these films and others like them, one must account for the aesthetic commitments that are embedded in each of these films. Film is a medium that can instantiate layers and layers of meanings and

44 This statement is not made to argue that respect and restraint would have universally characterized Evangelical engagement with the culture in previous years either. We have noted that this cultural and doctrinal bellicosity represents a strain of thought and commitment that has existed within Evangelicalism since the Second Great Awakening. This statement is simply made to recognize the more combative cultural and doctrinal (and perhaps even aesthetic) disposition that both funded the creation of this film, and then was subsequently funded by the aesthetic commitments of this film.

45 Leo Hott, "God Is Not Dead He Is Very Busy Right Now!!!!," review of *God's Not Dead*, Amazon, February 13, 2018, accessed July 27, 2024, https://www.amazon.com/gp/customer-reviews/R1PBSP4NGXLF4Y/.

aesthetic commitments within its images, sounds, and narratives, compressing and stacking them, allowing the viewer to take them all in within a single audio-visual stream. This aesthetic layering represents the affective alchemy that is film. Something similar can be said of the affections and practices that enact these aesthetic commitments as they have become embedded in the affections, dispositions, and imaginations of these film's audiences. They layer and stack these commitments into their own sets of dramatic performances of these commitments.

The practices funded by its aesthetic commitments to the shape of marriage highlight this process as it relates to *Fireproof*. In Mazdaprobegt's assertion, "As a man, I try to watch it once in a while to remind myself how to treat the love of my life,"[46] there are a set of practices, the periodic watching of the film, that underwrite a vision of Evangelical masculinity, and by extension its vision of Evangelical femininity as well. He appears to be returning specifically to imbibe and re-rehearse the aesthetic representations of each as they are embedded in the film. These representations are fundamentally essentialist, committed to a particular set of significations and meanings embedded in the bodies of each of the sexes. This includes the fundamental roles played by each in a marriage, with the husband enacting the mantle of leadership, fundamentally correlated to the sex of his body, and his wife and family submitting to that leadership. Here he returns to re-rehearse these aesthetic commitments, "to remind myself how to treat the love of my life"[47] and how best to enact them.

These aesthetic commitments to these particularities of the essentialist framing of male and female also become fundamentally related to individuals' and communities' devotional practices. Here a reviewer who identifies herself only as Heather notes, "This movie saved my marriage along with each of us doing the love dare. We have faced cheating and infidelity, the works. This movie woke us up to

46 Mazdaprobegt, "To the haters . . ."

47 Mazdaprobegt, "To the haters . . ."

where we were in our marriage and got us back on track. Both of us cried in the movie theater when it first came out and another pastor couple watching the movie prayed over us."[48] The intermingling of this couple's affective response to the film that leads to later practices offers insight into the affective engagement of their imaginations has an almost immediate and relatively sustained effect on their practices. They return both to their commitments to one another, and to what is framed as the proper aesthetic shape of marriage instantiated in *The Love Dare*.

The commitment to this essentialist aesthetic shape of marriage embedded in the practices of the audience are present in the review of SW VA Gal and her use of *Fireproof* and its related study materials as her Bible study group's devotional text. Of this experience she writes, "This was truly one of the best 'Bible' study classes I have attended. There is nothing on earth as important as your relationship with God and your spouse. If you put God first in your life, He will help you with your problems. He will heal your wounds, and that feeling of teenage puppy love will come back to a 15 year marriage. I am living proof of that after this movie and program!"[49] The association of the aesthetic commitments embedded in *Fireproof* were significant in her relationship to God and spouse respectively and "putting God first in your life."[50] Within this framework there is a paralleling of one's commitment to God and one's affective engagement and embrace of these particular essentialist aesthetic commitments embedded in *Fireproof*. Each of these reviewers reveals the affective, imaginative embrace of these aesthetic commitments to the reviewers' dramatic rendering of these commitments in their practices.

The aesthetic commitment that is most prominent in *God's Not Dead* is its commitment to the rational credibility of Christianity and the privileging of the spiritual over the material. The film's aesthetic

48 Heather, "Life Changing," review of *Fireproof*, Amazon.com, December 7, 2010, accessed July 27, 2024, https://www.amazon.com/gp/customer-reviews/R35ZG7U9OCNIVP/.

49 SW VA Gal, "Excellent Film for Couples."

50 SW VA Gal, "Excellent Film for Couples."

commitment to Christianity's rational credibility is the most authentic expression of the faith and those commitments become dramatically rendered in the practices of the film's audience. Through each, one can trace the formational line between the individual's engagement of the film's aesthetic commitments, and the ways in which those commitments become embodied in the viewer's and community's practices. In lisafrance-25224's review of the film, she noted, "This movie made me cry, it is so powerful down to the ending. I watched it twice, and will probably watch it a few more times to learn how to better defend my faith when questioned."[51] The viewer has affectively engaged the film and seems to have embraced the film's basic aesthetic commitment to the rational defense of Christianity as a fundamental good, representing a commitment central of the Christian good life. She notes that she has watched the film several times and plans to view it many more for the purposes of learning how to better defend the rational credibility of Christianity. The film then has not only shaped her viewing practices but has worked to form her devotional practices as well, as she desires to improve her ability to and increase her practice of defending the credibility of Christianity as a fundamental expression of her faith. Different viewers bring different degrees of intensity to these commitments and practices. Some include notes of grievance in their commitment to defend the credibility of Christianity.

An example of this is itskervin's review of the film in IMDB: "This movie inspired me greatly to be strong in my Faith and to defend him. For some time, its [*sic*] been difficult for me to try and defend God because of the people I surround myself with"[52] Here this reviewer has affectedly engaged and embraced the film's central aesthetic commitment and has amended his practices so that he can render that commitment visible both in word and deed to the people he surrounds himself with. He goes on to note the depth of the extent to which the film's aesthetic commitments have engaged

51 Lisafrance-25224, "I Basically created IMDB."

52 Itskervin, "Beautiful Movie."

his imagination and his practices, writing, "Its [*sic*] upsetting at how people view God. Especially in this day and age. But its [*sic*] encouraging to know the're [*sic*] people in this world who will do there [*sic*] best to defend him against those who seeks [*sic*] to destroy ones faith in there [*sic*] life."[53] He notes that he has not only affectively embraced the commitment to the importance of the defense of the Christianity's credibility, but has apparently also adopted some of his interpretive community's aesthetic commitments as well. There is a sense of grievance in his incredulity at the manner in which people view God "in this day and age," and a sense of the experience of being snubbed or mistreated as a result of one's commitment to Christianity. This sense of grievance is closely associated with the impulse to defend the credibility of Christianity and thus the impulse to defend Christians from and against malevolent actors, those with the perceived intent on harming Evangelicals, represented in the film by Dr. Radisson. In this way the interpretive community represents the virtuous "us" standing against an unvirtuous "them." The interpretive community plays a substantial role in the practices that grow out of those affections as this reviewer is bringing that group's aesthetic commitments to bear.

A CINEMATIC ADDENDUM

These formational processes are active across the broad spectrum of Evangelical films. This is because Evangelical films are fundamentally meaning-making endeavors that are attempting to affectively render visible their aesthetic, doctrinal, and devotional commitments while simultaneously earnestly projecting what they perceive to be the eternal significance of those commitments. They desire, above all else, that the audience experiences the eternal weight, value, and consequences of those commitments as they play out in the lives of individuals and communities. This represents the "why" of

53 Itskervin, "Beautiful Movie."

Evangelical filmmaking. The "how," however, adapts to the prevailing aesthetics, practices, conversations, and technologies of the times in which the film is produced. We see this differentiation on the "how" in the differing aesthetic and narrative approaches in the two films we have spent time with here. That adaptation is ongoing and active in contemporary Evangelical film projects.

As an example this adaptive impulse can be seen in 2023's Alejandro Monteverde film *Sound of Freedom*, a film whose subject matter is child sex trafficking; the film was produced by a company that interestingly represents a complex Mormon-Evangelical partnership. The film is not concerned with the audience's conversion in the way that films like *Fireproof* and *God's Not Dead* are. However, it is concerned with the gospel, rooting its aesthetic commitments in Scriptures that frame the film's narrative and the shape of the world it presents.[54] The theme the film returns to time and again is "God's children are not for sale." *Sound of Freedom* represents a film that was produced with and for a community of Evangelicals who still feel the urgency of eternal significance of the stakes of life, but who

54 Early in the film, as the film's protagonist, Agent Tim Ballard, played by Jim Caviezel, is completing a sting on a child sex trafficker, he paraphrases Luke 17:2 and Matthew 18:6, telling the trafficker, "Better a millstone be hung around your neck, and you be cast into the sea, than you should ever hurt one of these little ones." (*Sound of Freedom*, directed by Alejandro Monteverde [Angel Studios, 2023], 22:20) The text of Luke 17:1–2 notes, "Jesus said to his disciples: 'Things that cause people to stumble are bound to come, but woe to anyone through whom they come. It would be better for them to be thrown into the sea with a millstone tied around their neck than to cause one of these little ones to stumble'" (NIV). While the film's use and paraphrase of this text does help to ground the film within a particular set of both aesthetic and theological commitments, it also takes liberties with the meaning of the scriptural text it is drawing on. The text represents a warning to those whose words or actions would motivate individuals to forsake their faith in God. While the evil represented by child sex trafficking might certainly inspire the question of theodicy, which has undercut the faith of many, this is not the way in which the film's script engages the text. It endeavors to draw a much more direct reference to hurting "little ones" directly.

are also endeavoring to account for its social consequences in the meantime as well, in the ways that they have been shaped to perceive.

One could argue something similar of Michael Apted's 2007 film *Amazing Grace* about member of the British parliament William Wilberforce's work to abolish race-based slavery in the British Empire in the eighteenth and nineteenth centuries. While the film was about Wilberforce's successful endeavors, it was also read within Evangelical communities of interpretation to instantiate analogical references to the conflict surrounding abortion in the United States as well.[55] While this interpretation is in no way necessitated by the film's narrative, this is what the audience's aesthetic formation had formed them to perceive. The breadth of the Evangelical aesthetic texts, including their liturgical experiences and the ways in which they were formed through their interactions with their particular communities of faith, had formed them in such a way that large numbers made similar analogical jumps. To use Parker's framing, they perceived a Christian in Wilberforce embodying an uncompromising faith that funded a particular social and political commitment and perceived the analogy to abortion. This represents a snapshot of the aesthetic processes that move from the formation of affections, imaginations, and dispositions and ends in the formation of the practices that are consistent with these aesthetic and theological commitments.

CONCLUSION

With both *Fireproof* and *God's Not Dead* we can trace the ways in which the aesthetic commitments embedded in these aesthetic texts engage and affect the viewer's loves, imaginations, and dispositions,

55 Parker notes, "After seeing the film, these audiences used its message of uncompromising faith and determination to fuel their socio-political stance against issues like abortion and stem cell research. Rather than fully participating in the effort to raise awareness of the still-present evils of slavery, they saw the film as an encouragement to continue their fight against other contemporary evils" (53).

and the ways in which these work to form the practices that the viewer embodies as a result. These are the processes in play forming Evangelicals affections and actions in the two films we have spent time with here. The films have participated in a process that has formed its audience's affections, imaginations, and action as they relate to marriage, conversion, and Christianity's credibility. They have served to deepen, broaden, and reinforce notions of Evangelical identity, aiding the audience in perceiving the aesthetic commitments and practices that constitute Evangelicalism. They have projected Evangelicalism as a brand into the affections of its audience, and the audience has come to own that brand in their affections, and their basic perceptions of the world. They have come to love the brand so much that they want to share it with others. This is the aesthetics of moral formation.

CHAPTER 8

Conclusion

> The products Christians consume shape the faith they inhabit. Today, what is meant by "conservative evangelical" is as much about culture as it is about theology.
>
> —Kobes Du Mez, *Jesus and John Wayne: How White Evangelicals Corrupted a Faith and Fractured a Nation*

Evangelicalism can be framed by its commitments to conversionism, biblicism, activism, and crucicentrism.[1] While this framing is helpful, it does not paint a fulsome portrait of the lived experiences of Evangelicals. American Evangelicalism, and in particular white American Evangelicalism, embodies associations with and commitments to conservative approaches to political conversations, anti-institutional dispositions, strong senses of individualism, traditional gender roles, a bellicose sense of masculinity, an affection for sentimentality, a set of dispositions that privilege cultural and technological appropriation, and a commitment to the vernacular articulation of these and other commitments. Of course, this too offers just a sketch of the depth and breadth of the lived experience of Evangelicals.

Through the aesthetic texts associated with OCC, K-LOVE, and Evangelical films, many of these descriptive elements of the

1 See David Bebbington, *Evangelicalism in Modern Britain: A History from the 1730s to the 1980s* (Routledge, 1993), 2–17.

Evangelical experience ring true; however, by noting the ways in which Evangelicals affectionately engage and make meaning of these texts, one can begin to trace the processes by which these descriptive elements become embedded in the affections, dispositions, imaginations, and practices of Evangelicals. For example, the dramatic enactments of aesthetic commitments to conversionism in each set of these aesthetic texts come to embed themselves in Evangelical affections and practices. This emphasis is directly instantiated in the films *Fireproof* and *God's Not Dead* and in much of the music, commentary, and devotional spots on K-Love. This emphasis on conversion underwrites the entire reason for OCC's existence. Christmas shoeboxes are shipped to encourage the conversion of both its recipient and their families.

Running parallel to these texts' aesthetic commitments to conversionism, both the aesthetic texts associated with OCC and the two films also afforded a privileged place to the spiritual and the immaterial over and against the materiality of creation, framing salvation in an almost exclusively then-and-there fashion with significantly less concern to its material effects in the here and now. These aesthetic commitments and the affections, dispositions, and practices that they fund and that subsequently support them can be directly interlaced with this Evangelical commitment to conversionism. Furthermore, they offer insight into the aesthetic shape and core of these commitments. The Evangelical commitment to the importance of conversion generally emphasizes a notion of a salvation that frames an eternal future experienced after the end of this life as the ultimate good, and the most fulsome picture of the good life. For the grassroots Evangelical imagination, this represents the telos of faith in Jesus Christ. This framing of the good life then fundamentally de-emphasizes the importance and significance of the material experiences associated with embodied life and the material conditions that make life possible, in all its associated pleasure and suffering. Notions of the good and the practices that enact that good life are conformed to the perceived good of that telos. This aesthetic commitment privileging the spiritual over the material then represents one of the ways in which the Evangelical commitment to conversionism works itself out aesthetically and consequently, as it is embedded in aesthetic texts, then works its way into Evangelical aesthetic commitments, affections, imaginations, and practices. The aesthetic materiality of present world is afforded far less importance than the preferred spiritual realities of the world to come.

This commitment to spirituality, interiority, and conversion play out in a different way, through the Evangelical affection for the affective emotive embodiment associated with Pentecostally influenced worship experiences. This affection for affective emotive embodiment can also be associated with the affection for sentimentality that is often associated with the Evangelical experience. Todd Brenneman asserts, "Evangelicals are replicating a culture of emotionality . . . with almost every book or album they produce, implanting sentimentality in the lived experience of consumers who read the book, listen to the music, or watch the video."[2] Here, affections easily shape dispositions that then shape practices as worshippers translate the interiority of their affections directly into the employment of their bodies for the purposes of enacting Pentecostally shaped worship practices. This is related to the emphasis on interior experiences as an authenticator of one's conversion and a life of genuine faith. Both the emphasis on affective emotive embodiment and sentimentality plays out simultaneously in K-Love listeners' testimonies as they relate to the songs of worship and testimony broadcast by K-Love. This also speaks to the broad Pentecostalization of Evangelicalism that can be seen in its embrace of the affective emotive embodiment associated with popular worship music and contemporary Evangelical liturgies.

These formational processes also shape Evangelical dispositions as they work into broader cultural and political practices and commitments. As an example, *God's Not Dead* commits to articulating the rational credibility of Christianity within the context of popular culture. Within this framework the film's emphasis on this, and in particular the rational credibility of Evangelical Christianity, grows

2 Brenneman, *Homespun Gospel*, 14.

out of the strong individualism, anti-institutional dispositions, and politically conservative commitments that many of the Evangelical scholars polled earlier recognized as fundamental expressions of American Evangelicalism. These aesthetic and dispositional commitments are embedded not only in the rational case made by the film, but the aesthetic, emotive manner in which it makes that case. As such, the film represents something between an aesthetic response to the Evangelical community's perceptions of marginalization by and even exclusion from the exercising of their agency as a full participant in the popular culture, on one hand, and the aesthetic filing of a grievance against the broad popular culture for its marginalization on the other.

In addition, Evangelicalism has an affection for traditional gender roles and a bellicose masculinity. These affections are particularly present in the narrative of *Fireproof* and its commitment to an essentialist masculinity and femininity. The ways in which these affections worked their ways into many of the film's audience's cultural perceptions and practices shapes their aesthetic, devotional, and even political commitments. Through the films, these devotional, doctrinal, and political commitments are embedded in these aesthetic texts, working then to form the affections, imagination, and the aesthetic commitments of their audiences. Embedding these devotional, doctrinal, and political commitments in these aesthetic texts then funds the continuation of the aesthetic formational circle.

So then, the question still stands as to whether these Evangelical aesthetic formations represent the formations of virtues, vices, or both. Christian virtues (for example: faith, hope, love, persistence, kindness, temperance, chastity) are clearly present in each of the sets of aesthetic texts we have engaged. Furthermore, the Evangelical enactment of those virtues are at least partially rooted in the aesthetic formation and practices encouraged by each. However, the aesthetic nature of formation can also enable counter- or malformation.[3] This

3 Here we remember Willie James Jennings's account of the aesthetic processes that underwrote the white supremacy foundational to the European

potential malformation is at least partially rooted in the tensions that exist between the rational articulation of a particular meaning (say a theological doctrine) and the meaning instantiated in a particular aesthetic text, piece of material culture, or practice. Within this aesthetically formational framework, the meaning instantiated in the aesthetic text or practice will consistently prove more influential as it relates to the formation of affections, dispositions, and actions than a rational articulation will. Stated more succinctly, the aesthetic shape of a devotional, ethical, or political commitment that is embedded in a particular aesthetic text will do more to form an individual or community's beliefs, affections, dispositions, imaginations, and ultimately their practices than a solely rational articulation of the same doctrine.[4]

To that end there is a fundamental connection between aesthetic texts and the performances related to those texts. The dramatic performances of practices represent the performance of the aesthetic commitments that are embedded in those texts and pieces of material culture. In addition, because each aesthetic text instantiates a particular vision of the good life, and in the cases of OCC, K-Love, and Evangelical films, instantiates the framing of a particular set of

---

colonial projects and its ongoing persistence within contemporary affections, imaginations, and dispositions.

4 Rational articulations by their nature (for better or worse) are designed to minimize the affect the emotions play as it relates to persuasion. By minimizing the persuasional role of the emotions, rationality-centric approaches intend to bypass the affections and thus the body as a locus of persuasion. This effort to marginalize the role of the affections and the body in the process of spiritual and moral formation is itself a reflection and a performance of particular set of aesthetic and theological commitments that locate the core of humanity's fallenness or sinfulness in the body, and the desires the body generates. By extension this fallenness also extends into the affections and emotions of the individual. Here the rational is understood as a tool that is able to compensate for portions of this fallenness because it is thought to mitigate the influences of the body. (Theologian Malcolm Guite addresses just this type of thought process in his introduction to his book *Faith, Hope and Poetry: Theology and the Poetic Imagination* [Ashgate, 2010]. In particular see pages 10–11.) However, as I noted earlier, based on Mark Johnson's work, this privilege afforded to the rational is likely not entirely warranted as human rationality is as embedded in the senses and the body as the emotions are. See *The Meaning of the Body*, 55–59.

approaches to Christian discipleship as the good life, the practices and actions embodied by those who engage these texts represent performances of particular understandings or visions of the good life that are embedded in each. In short, the practices and actions taken by the audiences of these texts reveal which of the aesthetic commitments that are embedded in these texts have taken root in their affections, imaginations, and dispositions.

Stanley Hauerwas touches on this when he argues that character is a gift from the community. He argues that Christians attract others to God's story as they perform that story in their common life.[5] This attraction is true both for those who are members of the Christian community as Hauerwas envisions it, and for those outside of that community. This is ultimately why he argues that character is gift from the community.[6] As the Christian (or non-Christian outside of the community of faith) observes the performances of other Christians, that performance behaves as its own aesthetic text, working to form the affections and imaginations of the ones engaging that performance.[7] Thus, performance is not just an expression of the aesthetic formation that has occurred in an individual or community; it is also contributing to the further aesthetic formation of the community. Here practices are as aesthetically fundamental as the aesthetic texts themselves in the process of aesthetic formation.

An aesthetic approach to formation understands the rational and emotional, or perhaps better, the mind and the body, to be a unified whole. Therefore, it endeavors to engage the body and the affections while simultaneously engaging the rational, propositional, and doctrinal. It also recognizes the fundamental influence these processes

5 Hauerwas, *The Peaceable Kingdom*, 44.

6 Hauerwas, *The Peaceable Kingdom*, 45.

7 On a side note, this is something similar to what Paul is describing in 2 Corinthians 3 when he writes, "You are our epistle written in our hearts, known and read by all men; clearly you are an epistle of Christ, ministered by us, written not with ink but by the Spirit of the living God, not on tablets of stone but on tablets of flesh, that is, of the heart" (2 Cor 3:2–3 NKJV). Paul is writing of the persuasive power of bodies and performance.

play in forming both individual and community practices. Thus, the question of whether Evangelical aesthetic formation represents the formation of virtue or vice is heavily dependent upon both the aesthetic shape those Christian virtues take in each aesthetic text and the shape of the practices they fund.

For example, as one recognizes the formational effect Evangelical aesthetic texts assert as that text relates to the relationship of the materiality of creation and the spirituality that exists outside of time and space associated with Evangelical notions of salvation, the judgment of whether the Evangelical practices funded by these doctrinal and aesthetic commitments represent virtues or vices become dependent upon both the formation of the individual or community making that judgment and the formation of their perceptions. One's Christian aesthetic formation might dispose one to recognize a broadly experienced human thriving in the materiality of the commons, that is as a broadly experienced outgrowth of a Christian vision of the common good, as a virtue. Here one would perceive widely distributed experiences of cultural thriving and well-being as a fundamental good, regardless of the doctrinal, political, or cultural commitments of those who are thriving. However, one's Christian aesthetic formation might perceive this notion of human thriving as a common good only if it is rooted in the particularities of each individual's experience of and commitment to doctrinal and aesthetic commitments to an exclusively spiritual framing of salvation. Here one would not perceive broad cultural experiences of thriving as a fundamental good, as they are not directly rooted in the best good. In other words, Evangelical aesthetic commitments and visions of the good life might not allow for the perception of a broadly defined common good as a fundamental good, and thus might frame it as a vice, not a virtue.[8] The answer then as to whether these aesthetic formations represent the formation of Evangelical virtue or vice is

8 I would suggest we can witness commitments like this in play among those who advocate for the governing of the United States as a Christian nation, and in the rise of Christian Nationalism.

that they must fundamentally represent both. In each of the descriptive elements we have named here, one's understanding of each as either virtuous or immoral will be dependent upon the perceptions formed through the processes of aesthetic formation. One's perception of what constitutes virtue and what constitutes vice is directly related to one's aesthetic formation.

This also means that the aesthetic must play a fundamental role in any endeavors to persuade humans broadly and Evangelicals specifically of other approaches to faith and practice, or virtue and vice. We had noted the considerable apparent changes to Evangelical affections and practices since the days of the Moral Majority in the 1980s. The observations of these changes were framed around their broad support of Donald Trump and the ascent of Christian Nationalism, though as we have accounted for Evangelicalism's descriptive elements and the role aesthetics have played in the formation of Evangelical affections, dispositions, and practices as they relate to those elements, we might be able to recognize bits of the contemporary expressions of American Evangelicalism within those older sets of aesthetic texts and practices.

If the aesthetic processes of formation that have been described here represent even a partially accurate account of both broadly human and specifically Evangelical formation, then Evangelicals did not arrive at their devotional, doctrinal, political, and aesthetic commitments by fundamentally rational means. Recall the parishioner confronting his pastor after his sermon on Jesus's teaching to turn the other cheek, telling him, "Yes, but that doesn't work anymore. That's weak."[9] If the aesthetic account of formation offers an accurate picture of these different strands of development, then this parishioner did not arrive at his commitments regarding Jesus by exclusively rational means. This means that he and other Evangelicals cannot be argued out of their commitments. Reason alone will never shape that which one loves.

9 Detrow, Sánchez, and Handel, "He Was a Top Church Official."

If Evangelicals as humans are formed through aesthetic means, then any attempts to influence Evangelical affections, dispositions, and practices must be accomplished through aesthetic means. We can engage Evangelical aesthetic texts to understand the aesthetic commitments that have formed Evangelical affections and imaginations; however, if one wishes to engage individual Evangelicals or Evangelical communities to contest popular Evangelical notions of the good life and the practices that flow from that telos, one must renarrate and reframe the aesthetic commitments that fund those practices in ways that harness and refocus already existing affections, imaginations, and aesthetic commitments. As the formation of Evangelicals to this point in history has been accomplished by aesthetic means, so all future formation will also be accomplished by the same means.

Bibliography

Aristotle. *Aristotle's Poetics*. Translated by George Whalley, John Baxter, and Patrick Atherton. McGill-Queen's University Press, 1997.

Aristotle. *The Ethics of Aristotle: The Nicomachean Ethics*. Translated by J. A. K. Thomson. Penguin Classics, 1955.

Bebbington, David. *Evangelicalism in Modern Britain: A History from the 1730s to the 1980s*. Routledge, 1993.

Bourdieu, Pierre. *Distinction: A Social Critique of the Judgement of Taste*. Translated by Richard Nice. Harvard University Press, 1984.

Brenneman, Todd. *Homespun Gospel: The Triumph of Sentimentality in Contemporary American Evangelicalism*. Oxford University Press, 2014.

Brenneman, Todd. "Traveling Light: Max Lucado and the Power of Sentimentality in American Evangelicalism." PhD diss., The Florida State University, 2009.

Buschart, W. David. *Exploring Protestant Traditions: An Invitation to Theological Hospitality*. IVP Academic, 2006.

Conrad, Joseph. *The N***** of the Narcissus*. 1898. Available from https://www.gutenberg.org/cache/epub/17731/pg17731-images.html.

Craigo-Snell, Shannon. *The Empty Church: Theater, Theology and Bodily Hope*. Oxford University Press, 2014.

Dyrness, William. *The Earth Is God's: A Theology of American Culture*. Wipf & Stock Publishers, 1997.

Dyrness, William. *Poetic Theology: God and the Poetics of Everyday Life*. William B. Eerdman's Publishing Company, 2011.

Dyrness, William. *Reformed Theology and Visual Culture*. Cambridge University Press, 2004.

Dyrness, William. *Senses of the Soul: Art and the Visual in Christian Worship*. Cascade Books, 2008.

Fitzgerald, Francis. *The Evangelicals: The Struggle to Shape America*. Simon & Schuster, 2017.

Fodor, Jim. "The Play of Christian Life: When Wisdom Calls to Wisdom." In *Theatrical Theology: Explorations in Performing the Faith*, edited by Wesley Vander Lugt and Trevor Hart. Cascade Books, 2014.

Gadamer, Hans-Georg. *The Relevance of the Beautiful and Other Essays*. Edited by Robert Bernasconi. Cambridge University Press, 1986.

Graham, Franklin. *Rebel with a Cause: Finally Comfortable Being Graham; An Autobiography*. Thomas Nelson, Inc., 1995.

Graham, Franklin, and Estelle Condra. Illustrated by Dilleen Marsh. *Miracle in a Shoe Box: A Christmas Gift of Wonder*. Thomas Nelson, 1995.

Guite, Malcolm. *Faith, Hope and Poetry: Theology and the Poetic Imagination*. Ashgate Publishing, 2010.

Harris, Max. *Theatre and Incarnation*. William B. Eerdmans Publishing Company, 1990.

Hart, Trevor. "Beyond Theatre and Incarnation." In *Theatrical Theology: Explorations in Performing the Faith*, edited by Wesley Vander Lugt and Trevor Hart. Cascade Books, 2014.

Hatch, Nathan O. *The Democratization of American Christianity*. Yale University Press, 1989.

Hauerwas, Stanley. *A Community of Character: Toward a Constructive Christian Social Ethic*. University of Notre Dame Press, 1981.

Hauerwas, Stanley. *The Peaceable Kingdom: A Primer in Christian Ethics*. University of Notre Dame Press, 1983.

Hauerwas, Stanley. *Performing the Faith: Bonhoeffer and the Practice of Nonviolence*. Wipf and Stock Publishers, 2004.

Hauerwas, Stanley, and Charles Pinches. *Christians among the Virtues*. University of Notre Dame Press 1997.

Hawkins, Peter. *Danté's Testaments: Essays on Scripture Imagination*. Stanford University Press, 1999.

Herdt, Jennifer A. *Putting on Virtue: The Legacy of the Splendid Vices*. The University of Chicago Press, 2008.

Jennings, Willie James. *The Christian Imagination: Theology and the Origins of Race*. Yale University Press, 2010.

Johnson, Mark. *The Meaning of the Body: Aesthetics of Human Understanding*. The University of Chicago Press, 2007.

Johnson, Todd E. "Doing God's Story: Theatre, Christian Initiation, and Being Human Together." In *Theatrical Theology: Explorations in Performing the Faith*, edited by Wesley Vander Lugt and Trevor Hart. Cascade Books, 2014.

Johnson, Todd Eric, and Dale Savidge. *Performing the Sacred: Theology and Theatre in Dialogue*. Baker Academic, 2009.

Kant, Immanuel. *Critique of Judgment*. Edited by Nicholas Walker. Translated by James Creed Meredith. Oxford University Press, 2007.

Kobes Du Mez, Kristin. *Jesus and John Wayne: How White Evangelicals Corrupted a Faith and Fractured a Nation*. Liveright Publishing Corporation, 2020.

Kotva, Joseph J., Jr. *The Christian Case for Virtue Ethics*. Georgetown University Press, 1996.

Levine, Lawrence W. *Highbrow/Lowbrow: The Emergence of Cultural Hierarchy in America*. Harvard University Press, 1988.

Lim, Swee Hung, and Lester Ruth. *Lovin' on Jesus: A Concise History of Contemporary Worship*. Abingdon Press, 2017.

Lindvall, Terry, and Andrew Quicke. *Celluloid Sermons: The Emergence of the Christian Film Industry, 1930–1986*. New York University Press, 2011.

Lyotard, Jean François. "Gesture and Commentary." In *Between Ethics and Aesthetics: Crossing the Boundaries*, edited by Dorata Glowacka and Stephen Boos. State University of New York Press, 2002.

MacIntyre, Alasdair. *After Virtue: A Study in Moral Theory*. University of Notre Dame Press, 1984.

Morgan, David. *The Embodied Eye: Religious Visual Culture and the Social Life of Feeling*. University of California Press, 2012.

Morgan, David. "Protestant Visual Piety and the Aesthetics of American Mass Culture." In *Mediating Religion*, edited by Jolyon Mitchell and Sophia Marriage. T&T Clark, 2003.

Morgan, David. *The Sacred Gaze: Religious Visual Culture in Theory and Practice*. University of California Press, 2004.

Mulvey, Laura. "Visual Pleasure and Narrative Cinema." *Screen*, 16, no. 3 (Autumn 1975).

Nussbaum, Martha. *Love's Knowledge: Essays on Philosophy and Literature*. Oxford University Press, 1990.

O'Connor, Flannery. *Mystery and Manners: Occasional Prose*. Edited by Sally Fitzgerald and Robert Fitzgerald. Farrar, Straus & Giroux, 1969.

Parker, J. Ryan. *Cinema as Pulpit: Sherwood Pictures and the Church Film Movement*. McFarland & Co., Inc., 2012.

Payne, Leah. *God Gave Rock & Roll to You: A History of Contemporary Christian Music*. Oxford University Press, 2023.

Rivera, Mayra. *Poetics of the Flesh*. Duke University Press, 2015.

Smith, Adam. *The Theory of Moral Sentiments*. Amazon Publishing, 2016.

Smith, James K. A. *Imagining the Kingdom: How Worship Works*. Vol. 2 of *Cultural Liturgies*. Baker Academic, 2013.

Smith, James K. A. *Thinking in Tongues: Pentecostal Contributions to Christian Philosophy*. Eerdmans Publishing, 2010.

Smith, James K. A. *You Are What You Love: The Spiritual Power of Habit*. Brazos Press, 2016.

Stackhouse, John G. *Evangelicalism: A Very Short Introduction*. Oxford University Press, 2022.

Thornton, Katie. "Jesus Take the Dial." *Rolling Stone*. February 2024.

Vanhoozer, Kevin. *Faith Speaking Understanding: Performing the Drama of Doctrine*. Westminster John Knox Press, 2014.

Viladesau, Richard. "Aesthetics and Religion." In *The Oxford Handbook of Religion and the Arts*, edited by Frank Burch Brown. Oxford University Press, 2014.

Von Balthasar, Hans Urs. *Love Alone Is Credible*. Translated by D.C. Schindler. Ignatius Press, 1963.

Von Balthasar, Hans Urs. *The Glory of the Lord: A Theological Aesthetics*. Vol. 1, *Seeing the Form*. Translated by Erasmo Leiva-Merkakis. Ignatius Press, 1982.

Von Balthasar, Hans Urs. *Theo-Drama: Theological Dramatic Theory*. Vol. 1, *Prolegomena*. Translated by Graham Harrison. Ignatius Press, 1983.

Vredenburgh, Steven. "Evangelizing Atheism: Missing the Mark in Recent Christian Film." *Christian Scholars Review* 50, no. 1 (Fall 2020).

Ward, Pete. "Affective Alliance or Circuits of Power: The Production and Consumption of Contemporary Charismatic Worship in Britain." *International Journal of Practical Theology* 9, no. 1 (2005): 25–39.

Wells, Sam. *Improvisation: The Drama of Christian Ethics*. Brazos Press, 2004.

Yong, Amos. *The Future of Evangelical Theology: Soundings from the Asian American Diaspora*. IVP Academic, 2014.

Index